The Heavens Were Opened

The Heavens Were Opened

Joseph Smith's First Vision

Jay A. Parry

STONEWELL PRESS

ISBN 978-1-62730-122-0

Published by Stonewell Press

Salt Lake City, UT

CONTENTS

INTRODUCTION

In the spring of 1820, the most important event in two thousand years occurred in a small village in New York. A young farm boy with a common name, Joseph Smith, had a remarkable vision of God the Father and His Son, Jesus Christ. He was poorly educated in the things of the world, but he was pure and innocent, with a yearning heart and a questing mind. He was thirsty for knowledge of the things of God. Rather than receiving formal schooling, Joseph was tutored by God's Spirit, by angels, and by God Himself. In the process, he was gradually prepared to be the founding prophet of the great dispensation established to prepare the world for the Second Coming of Christ.

That vision literally changed the world. Once the heavens had opened again, the Lord began to pour forth a flood of blessings upon his children on the earth. Joseph Smith became the instrument through which priesthood keys were bestowed, God's word was revealed in abundance, and ordinances and covenants were restored. Through the gift and power of God, Joseph translated the Book of Mormon: Another Testament of Jesus Christ from an ancient tongue, and, directed by God, he organized a church after the pattern of the New Testament church. God directed that he name the church after the Savior who heads that church: The Church of Jesus Christ of Latter-day Saints.

Then, when only thirty-eight years old, he died a martyr's death, sealing with blood his testimony of all the heavenly gifts and powers he had received.

Two centuries have passed since the day Joseph walked into an ordinary grove of trees near his home. His following grew from six people to six hundred to six hundred thousand. The church he established now has more than 16 million members in more than 160 countries. Nearly 200 million copies of the Book of Mormon have been distributed in 110 languages. (This number is extrapolated from the figure given in *Ensign,* Mar. 2010, 74.)

The ancient prophet Daniel interpreted a strange dream his king had experienced. He saw a great stone that rolled down a mountain, breaking apart the kingdoms of the world, and then filling the entire earth. That stone, Daniel said, represented the work of God. "The God of heaven [would] set up a kingdom, which shall never be destroyed: . . . and it shall stand forever." (Dan. 2:31–45.)

Some twenty-five hundred years after Daniel uttered his prophecy, it was fulfilled through Joseph Smith. The "God of heaven" began to set up his latter-day kingdom in 1820, when He appeared to the boy Joseph in the grove. The stone is rolling down the mountain, and God's kingdom is filling the world. Surely, as Daniel said, that kingdom "shall stand forever."

This book focuses on the world-tilting moment when the boy Joseph received his marvelous vision. Part 1 includes the accounts of the vision Joseph shared personally during his lifetime. It also includes a single-narrative harmony of those accounts, editorially blending them into one. Part 2 collects a number of reminiscences of those who knew the Prophet Joseph, recounting the circumstances of the vision as they had heard it during his lifetime. Part 3 brings together testimonies and teachings about the First Vision that were uttered by prophets and apostles of the following generations. And Part 4 shares additional teachings, giving further insight into the glorious event that took place on that beautiful spring day in 1820.

Part 1

JOSEPH SMITH'S ACCOUNTS

In 1820, a fourteen-year-old boy witnessed a most amazing vision—an actual visit from both God the Father and His Son, Jesus Christ. That boy, Joseph Smith, made a pointed comment to his mother that same day, telling her that he had learned for himself that the church she had recently joined was not true. The record does not tell us how much else he told her—or how much he told his family at that time. He may have been afraid that they would not believe his incredible story. After the visit of the angel Moroni three years later, Joseph hesitated to tell his father about it, saying, "I was afraid my father would not believe me." To that, Moroni responded, "He will believe every word you say to him." (B. H. Roberts, *Comprehensive History of the Church*, 1:75.) True to the promise, when Joseph Sr. heard Joseph's account of Moroni's visit, he said that "it was of God." (JS–History 1:50.)

We do know that Joseph told a local minister about his 1820 vision. Unfortunately, the minister was far less open than Joseph Sr. later proved to be. "He treated my communication not only lightly, but with great contempt, saying it was all of the devil." (JS–Matt. 1:21.) Others followed suit; Joseph became the subject of "a great deal of prejudice"; local preachers sought to "excite the public mind against me, and create a bitter persecution." (JS–Matt. 1:22.)

Perhaps because of that highly negative response, or perhaps because Joseph did not yet feel confident in his ability to express himself in writing (or both), he did not immediately record his experience. (The absence of an early record, however, does not mean that such a record was not created. The Smith family lived in difficult circumstances on the frontier. Further, the family was forced to move from place to place throughout the life of Joseph Smith Jr. It's possible that any early record Joseph created was lost or destroyed.)

Or perhaps he was restrained by the Spirit, with the Lord telling him it was not yet time to share and/or record the vision. Importantly, in Joseph's 1838 account, he mentions this very issue: "many other things did he say unto me, which I cannot write at this time." (JS—Matthew 1:20. For prophetic precedents of this principle, see Acts 16:6; 1 Nephi 14:25, 28; Alma 12:9–11; see also D&C 63:64.) The Savior himself told his followers to be careful about how they share that which is sacred: "Give not that which is holy unto the dogs, neither cast ye your pearls before swine, lest they trample them under their feet, and turn again and rend you." (Matthew 7:6.) The response Joseph received from the local preachers may have reinforced this injunction in his mind.

Joseph Smith made his first (that we know of) written record of the First Vision in 1832. This is the only account in his own handwriting. In November 1835, he shared his experience with a visitor to Kirtland, Ohio; this was recorded by one of his scribes, Warren Parrish. In 1838, Joseph gave the longest version of the vision, again recorded by scribes. This was intended to be part of the official history of the Church and is the version that is included in the Pearl of Great Price. Then in 1842, Joseph included an account of the First Vision as part of what is known as the Wentworth letter, written to be published in a Chicago newspaper.

The different accounts of the vision emphasize different things. This is to be expected rather than surprising. It is a common trait of human memory to recount an event—even a life-changing event—in different ways at different times to different people. There are three accounts of Paul's life-defining experience on the road to Damascus—and they differ in important details. (See Acts 9:3–8; 22:6–11; Acts 26:13–19.) The story of Jesus's transfiguration is recorded in the three Synoptic Gospels (Matthew 17:1–13; Mark 9:2–13; Luke 9:28–36), and again there are significant differences among the three accounts. Even more noteworthy, though, is the fact that John, who was the only Gospel writer who was an eyewitness of the event, never wrote of it at all! (Some scholars believe that John may have been making oblique references to the transfiguration in John 1:14 and 12:27–33, but these are decidedly ambiguous.)

President Gordon B. Hinckley wrote, "I am not worried that the Prophet Joseph Smith gave a number of versions of the first vision any more than I am worried that there are four different writers of the gospels in the New Testament, each with his own perceptions, each telling the events to meet his own purpose for writing at the time. I am more concerned with the fact that God has revealed in this dispensation a great and marvelous and beautiful plan that motivates men and women to love their Creator and their Redeemer, to appreciate and serve one another, to walk in faith on the road that leads to immortality and eternal life." (*Ensign*, Oct 1984, 2.)

This section presents five accounts of Joseph Smith's vision in chronological order. Spelling and punctuation have been standardized. In a few cases, paragraph breaks have been added to enhance readability. Following these accounts is a combined version, where the accounts are presented in a single narrative harmony. No harmony can be perfect, since it combines different writings created at different times. All the words in the harmony are Joseph Smith's, with the exception of a few that are enclosed in brackets. Also, in some cases it is impossible to know where a particular phrase should fit, which required editorial judgments. Still, despite any deficiencies, this harmony gives helpful insights into the remarkable experience of Joseph Smith in a grove that, in the process, became sacred.

The 1832 Handwritten Account

A history of the life of Joseph Smith Jr.; an account of his marvelous experience and of all the mighty acts which he doeth in the name of Jesus Christ, the son of the living God, of whom he beareth record; and also an account of the rise of the church of Christ in the eve of time according as the Lord brought forth and established by his hand: firstly, he receiving the testimony from on high; secondly, the ministering of angels; thirdly, the reception of the holy priesthood by the ministering of angels to administer the letter of the gospel—the law and commandments as they were given unto him—and the ordinances; fourthly, a confirmation and reception of the high priesthood after the holy order of the son of the living God, power and ordinance from on high to preach the gospel in the administration and demonstration of the spirit the keys of the kingdom of God, conferred upon him, and the continuation of the blessings of God to him &c—

I was born in the town of Sharon in the State of Vermont, North America, on the twenty-third day of December AD 1805 of goodly parents who spared no pains to instruct me in the Christian religion. At the age of about ten years my father, Joseph Smith Senior, moved to Palmyra, Ontario County in the state of New York. And being in indigent circumstances, they were obliged to labor hard for the support of a large family, having nine children. And as it required the exertions of all that were able to render any assistance for the support of the family, therefore we were deprived of the benefit of an education. Suffice it to say I was merely instructed in reading, writing, and the ground rules of arithmetic, which constituted my whole literary acquirements.

At about the age of twelve years, my mind become seriously impressed with regard to the all-important concerns for the welfare of my immortal soul, which led me to searching the scriptures—believing, as I was taught, that they contained the word of God and thus applying myself to them. My intimate acquaintance with those of different denominations led me to marvel exceedingly, for I discovered that they did not adorn their profession by a holy walk and godly conversation agreeable to what I found contained in that sacred depository. This was a grief to my soul.

Thus, from the age of twelve years to fifteen I pondered many things in my heart concerning the situation of the world of mankind, the contentions and divisions, the wickedness and abominations, and the darkness which pervaded the minds of mankind. My mind became exceedingly distressed, for I became convicted of my sins, and by searching the scriptures I found that mankind did not come unto the Lord but that they had apostatized from the true and living faith, and there was no society or denomination that was built upon the gospel of Jesus Christ as recorded in the New Testament. I felt to mourn for my own sins and for the sins of the world, for I learned in the scriptures that God was the same yesterday, today, and forever, that he was no respecter of persons, for he was God.

For I looked upon the sun, the glorious luminary of the earth, and also the moon, rolling in their majesty through the heavens, and also the stars shining in their courses, and the earth also upon which I stood, and the beasts of the field, and the fowls of heaven, and the fish of the waters, and also man walking forth upon the face of the earth in majesty and in the strength of beauty, whose power and intelligence in governing the things which are so exceedingly great and marvelous, even in the likeness of him who created them. And when I considered upon these things, my heart exclaimed, "Well hath the wise man said, 'It is a fool that saith in his heart, there is no God.'" My heart exclaimed, "All, all these bear testimony and bespeak an omnipotent and omnipresent power, a being who maketh laws and decreeth and bindeth all things in their bounds, who filleth eternity, who was and is and will be from all eternity to eternity." And I considered all these things and that that being seeketh such to worship him as worship him in spirit and in truth.

Therefore, I cried unto the Lord for mercy, for there was none else to whom I could go and obtain mercy. And the Lord heard my cry in the wilderness, and while in the attitude of calling upon the Lord, in the sixteenth year of my age, a pillar of light above the brightness of the sun at noonday came down from above and rested upon me. I was filled with the spirit of God, and the Lord opened the heavens upon me and I saw the Lord.

And he spake unto me, saying, "Joseph, my son, thy sins are forgiven thee. Go thy way, walk in my statutes, and keep my commandments. Behold, I am the Lord of glory. I was crucified for the world, that all those who believe on my name may have eternal life. Behold, the world lieth in sin at this time, and none doeth good, no, not one. They have turned aside from the gospel and keep not my commandments. They draw near to me with their lips while their hearts are far from me. And mine anger is kindling against the inhabitants of the earth, to visit them according to their ungodliness and to bring to pass that which hath been spoken by the mouth of the prophets and apostles. Behold and lo, I come quickly, as it is written of me, in the cloud, clothed in the glory of my Father."

My soul was filled with love, and for many days I could rejoice with great joy. The Lord was with me, but I could find none that would believe the heavenly vision. Nevertheless, I pondered these things in my heart. ("History, circa Summer 1832," p. 2, josephsmithpapers.org/paper-summary/history-circa-summer-1832/2. This account suggests that Joseph was fifteen years old, rather than fourteen, when he saw the vision. Since Joseph and his family apparently did not keep contemporaneous records, it is understandable that he may not have precisely remembered the exact time of the vision.)

The 1835 Journal Account

Being wrought up in my mind respecting the subject of religion, and looking at the different systems taught the children of men, I knew not who was right or who was wrong. And considering it of the first importance that I should be right in matters that involve eternal consequences, being thus perplexed in mind

I retired to the silent grove and bowed down before the Lord, under a realizing sense that he had said (if the Bible be true), "Ask, and you shall receive; knock, and it shall be opened; seek, and you shall find," and again, "If any man lack wisdom, let him ask of God, who giveth to all men liberally, and upbraideth not."

Information was what I most desired at this time, and with a fixed determination to obtain it, I called upon the Lord for the first time in the place above stated. Or in other words, I made a fruitless attempt to pray; my tongue seemed to be swollen in my mouth, so that I could not utter. I heard a noise behind me, like some person walking towards me. I strove again to pray but could not. The noise of walking seemed to draw nearer. I sprung up on my feet and looked around but saw no person or thing that was calculated to produce the noise of walking.

I kneeled again. My mouth was opened and my tongue liberated, and I called on the Lord in mighty prayer. A pillar of fire appeared above my head. It presently rested down upon me and filled me with joy unspeakable. A personage appeared in the midst of this pillar of flame, which was spread all around and yet nothing consumed. Another personage soon appeared, like unto the first. He said unto me, "Thy sins are forgiven thee." He testified unto me that Jesus Christ is the son of God. And I saw many angels in this vision. I was about fourteen years old when I received this first communication. ("Journal, 1835–1836," p. 23, josephsmithpapers.org/paper-summary/journal-1835-1836/24. This account was recorded on 9–11 Nov. 1835.)

The 1838 Canonized Account

1 Owing to the many reports which have been put in circulation by evil-disposed and designing persons, in relation to the rise and progress of The Church of Jesus Christ of Latter-day Saints, all of which have been designed by the authors thereof to militate against its character as a Church and its progress in the world—I have been induced to write this history, to

disabuse the public mind, and put all inquirers after truth in possession of the facts, as they have transpired, in relation both to myself and the Church, so far as I have such facts in my possession.

2 In this history I shall present the various events in relation to this Church, in truth and righteousness, as they have transpired, or as they at present exist, being now [1838] the eighth year since the organization of the said Church.

3 I was born in the year of our Lord one thousand eight hundred and five, on the twenty-third day of December, in the town of Sharon, Windsor county, State of Vermont. . . . My father, Joseph Smith, Sen., left the State of Vermont, and moved to Palmyra, Ontario (now Wayne) county, in the State of New York, when I was in my tenth year, or thereabouts. In about four years after my father's arrival in Palmyra, he moved with his family into Manchester in the same county of Ontario—

4 His family consisting of eleven souls, namely, my father, Joseph Smith; my mother, Lucy Smith (whose name, previous to her marriage, was Mack, daughter of Solomon Mack); my brothers, Alvin (who died November 19th, 1823, in the 26th year of his age), Hyrum, myself, Samuel Harrison, William, Don Carlos; and my sisters, Sophronia, Catherine, and Lucy.

5 Some time in the second year after our removal to Manchester, there was in the place where we lived an unusual excitement on the subject of religion. It commenced with the Methodists, but soon became general among all the sects in that region of country. Indeed, the whole district of country seemed affected by it, and great multitudes united themselves to the different religious parties, which created no small stir and division amongst the people, some crying, "Lo, here!" and others, "Lo, there!" Some were contending for the Methodist faith, some for the Presbyterian, and some for the Baptist.

6 For, notwithstanding the great love which the converts to these different faiths expressed at the time of their conversion, and the great zeal manifested by the respective clergy, who were active in getting up and promoting this extraordinary scene of religious feeling, in order to have everybody converted, as they

were pleased to call it, let them join what sect they pleased; yet when the converts began to file off, some to one party and some to another, it was seen that the seemingly good feelings of both the priests and the converts were more pretended than real; for a scene of great confusion and bad feeling ensued—priest contending against priest, and convert against convert; so that all their good feelings one for another, if they ever had any, were entirely lost in a strife of words and a contest about opinions.

7 I was at this time in my fifteenth year. My father's family was proselyted to the Presbyterian faith, and four of them joined that church, namely, my mother, Lucy; my brothers Hyrum and Samuel Harrison; and my sister Sophronia.

8 During this time of great excitement my mind was called up to serious reflection and great uneasiness; but though my feelings were deep and often poignant, still I kept myself aloof from all these parties, though I attended their several meetings as often as occasion would permit. In process of time my mind became somewhat partial to the Methodist sect, and I felt some desire to be united with them; but so great were the confusion and strife among the different denominations, that it was impossible for a person young as I was, and so unacquainted with men and things, to come to any certain conclusion who was right and who was wrong.

9 My mind at times was greatly excited, the cry and tumult were so great and incessant. The Presbyterians were most decided against the Baptists and Methodists, and used all the powers of both reason and sophistry to prove their errors, or, at least, to make the people think they were in error. On the other hand, the Baptists and Methodists in their turn were equally zealous in endeavoring to establish their own tenets and disprove all others.

10 In the midst of this war of words and tumult of opinions, I often said to myself: What is to be done? Who of all these parties are right; or, are they all wrong together? If any one of them be right, which is it, and how shall I know it?

11 While I was laboring under the extreme difficulties caused

by the contests of these parties of religionists, I was one day reading the Epistle of James, first chapter and fifth verse, which reads:
*If any of you lack wisdom, let him ask of God, that giveth to all men
liberally, and upbraideth not; and it shall be given him.*

12 Never did any passage of scripture come with more power
to the heart of man than this did at this time to mine. It seemed
to enter with great force into every feeling of my heart. I reflected
on it again and again, knowing that if any person needed wisdom
from God, I did; for how to act I did not know, and unless I could
get more wisdom than I then had, I would never know; for the
teachers of religion of the different sects understood the same
passages of scripture so differently as to destroy all confidence in
settling the question by an appeal to the Bible.

13 At length I came to the conclusion that I must either remain
in darkness and confusion, or else I must do as James directs, that
is, ask of God. I at length came to the determination to "ask of
God," concluding that if he gave wisdom to them that lacked wisdom, and would give liberally, and not upbraid, I might venture.

14 So, in accordance with this, my determination to ask of
God, I retired to the woods to make the attempt. It was on the
morning of a beautiful, clear day, early in the spring of eighteen
hundred and twenty. It was the first time in my life that I had
made such an attempt, for amidst all my anxieties I had never as
yet made the attempt to pray vocally.

15 After I had retired to the place where I had previously designed to go, having looked around me, and finding myself
alone, I kneeled down and began to offer up the desires of my
heart to God. I had scarcely done so, when immediately I was
seized upon by some power which entirely overcame me, and
had such an astonishing influence over me as to bind my tongue
so that I could not speak. Thick darkness gathered around me,
and it seemed to me for a time as if I were doomed to sudden destruction.

16 But, exerting all my powers to call upon God to deliver me
out of the power of this enemy which had seized upon me, and
at the very moment when I was ready to sink into despair and

abandon myself to destruction—not to an imaginary ruin, but to the power of some actual being from the unseen world, who had such marvelous power as I had never before felt in any being—just at this moment of great alarm, I saw a pillar of light exactly over my head, above the brightness of the sun, which descended gradually until it fell upon me.

17 It no sooner appeared than I found myself delivered from the enemy which held me bound. When the light rested upon me I saw two Personages, whose brightness and glory defy all description, standing above me in the air. One of them spake unto me, calling me by name and said, pointing to the other—*This is My Beloved Son. Hear Him!*

18 My object in going to inquire of the Lord was to know which of all the sects was right, that I might know which to join. No sooner, therefore, did I get possession of myself, so as to be able to speak, than I asked the Personages who stood above me in the light, which of all the sects was right (for at this time it had never entered into my heart that all were wrong)—and which I should join.

19 I was answered that I must join none of them, for they were all wrong; and the Personage who addressed me said that all their creeds were an abomination in his sight; that those professors were all corrupt; that: "they draw near to me with their lips, but their hearts are far from me, they teach for doctrines the commandments of men, having a form of godliness, but they deny the power thereof."

20 He again forbade me to join with any of them; and many other things did he say unto me, which I cannot write at this time. When I came to myself again, I found myself lying on my back, looking up into heaven. When the light had departed, I had no strength; but soon recovering in some degree, I went home. And as I leaned up to the fireplace, mother inquired what the matter was. I replied, "Never mind, all is well—I am well enough off." I then said to my mother, "I have learned for myself that Presbyterianism is not true." It seems as though the adversary was aware, at a very early period of my life, that I was destined to

prove a disturber and an annoyer of his kingdom; else why should the powers of darkness combine against me? Why the opposition and persecution that arose against me, almost in my infancy?

21 Some few days after I had this vision, I happened to be in company with one of the Methodist preachers, who was very active in the before mentioned religious excitement; and, conversing with him on the subject of religion, I took occasion to give him an account of the vision which I had had. I was greatly surprised at his behavior; he treated my communication not only lightly, but with great contempt, saying it was all of the devil, that there were no such things as visions or revelations in these days; that all such things had ceased with the apostles, and that there would never be any more of them.

22 I soon found, however, that my telling the story had excited a great deal of prejudice against me among professors of religion, and was the cause of great persecution, which continued to increase; and though I was an obscure boy, only between fourteen and fifteen years of age, and my circumstances in life such as to make a boy of no consequence in the world, yet men of high standing would take notice sufficient to excite the public mind against me, and create a bitter persecution; and this was common among all the sects—all united to persecute me.

23 It caused me serious reflection then, and often has since, how very strange it was that an obscure boy, of a little over fourteen years of age, and one, too, who was doomed to the necessity of obtaining a scanty maintenance by his daily labor, should be thought a character of sufficient importance to attract the attention of the great ones of the most popular sects of the day, and in a manner to create in them a spirit of the most bitter persecution and reviling. But strange or not, so it was, and it was often the cause of great sorrow to myself.

24 However, it was nevertheless a fact that I had beheld a vision. I have thought since, that I felt much like Paul, when he made his defense before King Agrippa, and related the account of the vision he had when he saw a light, and heard a voice; but still there were but few who believed him; some said he was

dishonest, others said he was mad; and he was ridiculed and reviled. But all this did not destroy the reality of his vision. He had seen a vision, he knew he had, and all the persecution under heaven could not make it otherwise; and though they should persecute him unto death, yet he knew, and would know to his latest breath, that he had both seen a light and heard a voice speaking unto him, and all the world could not make him think or believe otherwise.

25 So it was with me. I had actually seen a light, and in the midst of that light I saw two Personages, and they did in reality speak to me; and though I was hated and persecuted for saying that I had seen a vision, yet it was true; and while they were persecuting me, reviling me, and speaking all manner of evil against me falsely for so saying, I was led to say in my heart: Why persecute me for telling the truth? I have actually seen a vision; and who am I that I can withstand God, or why does the world think to make me deny what I have actually seen? For I had seen a vision; I knew it, and I knew that God knew it, and I could not deny it, neither dared I do it; at least I knew that by so doing I would offend God, and come under condemnation.

26 I had now got my mind satisfied so far as the sectarian world was concerned—that it was not my duty to join with any of them, but to continue as I was until further directed. I had found the testimony of James to be true—that a man who lacked wisdom might ask of God, and obtain, and not be upbraided. (JS–History 1:1–26. The original version of this account can be found at "History, 1838–1856, volume A-1 [23 December 1805–30 August 1834]," p. 4, josephsmithpapers.org/paper-summary /history-1838-1856-volume-a-1-23-december-1805-30-august-1834/4.)

The 1842 Wentworth Letter Account

I was born in the town of Sharon Windsor co., Vermont, on the 23d of December, a.d. 1805. When ten years old my parents removed to Palmyra New York, where we resided about four years, and from thence we removed to the town of Manchester.

My father was a farmer and taught me the art of husbandry. When about fourteen years of age, I began to reflect upon the importance of being prepared for a future state, and upon enquiring about the plan of salvation, I found that there was a great clash in religious sentiment; if I went to one society, they referred me to one plan, and another to another, each one pointing to his own particular creed as the summum bonum of perfection. Considering that all could not be right, and that God could not be the author of so much confusion, I determined to investigate the subject more fully, believing that if God had a church it would not be split up into factions, and that if he taught one society to worship one way, and administer in one set of ordinances, he would not teach another principles which were diametrically opposed. Believing the word of God, I had confidence in the declaration of James; "If any man lack wisdom, let him ask of God, who giveth to all men liberally and upbraideth not, and it shall be given him."

I retired to a secret place in a grove and began to call upon the Lord. While fervently engaged in supplication, my mind was taken away from the objects with which I was surrounded, and I was enwrapped in a heavenly vision and saw two glorious personages who exactly resembled each other in features and likeness, surrounded with a brilliant light which eclipsed the sun at noonday. They told me that all religious denominations were believing in incorrect doctrines and that none of them was acknowledged of God as his church and kingdom. And I was expressly commanded to "go not after them," at the same time receiving a promise that the fulness of the gospel should at some future time be made known unto me. ("'Church History,' 1 March 1842," p. 706, josephsmithpapers.org/ paper-summary/church-history-1-march-1842/1.)

The 1843 David Nye White Account

The Lord does reveal himself to me. I know it. He revealed himself to me first when I was about fourteen years old, a mere boy. I will tell you about it. There was a reformation among the different religious denominations in the neighborhood where I lived, and I became serious, and was desirous to know what Church to join. While thinking of this matter, I opened the Testament promiscuously on these words, in James, "Ask of the Lord who giveth to all men liberally and upbraideth not." I just determined I'd ask him.

I immediately went out into the woods where my father had a clearing, and went to the stump where I had stuck my axe when I had quit work, and I kneeled down, and prayed, saying, "O Lord, what Church shall I join."

Directly I saw a light, and then a glorious personage in the light, and then another personage, and the first personage said to the second, "Behold my beloved Son, hear him."

I then, addressed this second person, saying, "O Lord, what Church shall I join."

He replied, "Don't join any of them, they are all corrupt."

The vision then vanished, and when I come to myself, I was sprawling on my back; and it was sometime before my strength returned. When I went home and told the people that I had a revelation, and that all the churches were corrupt, they persecuted me, and they have persecuted me ever since. They thought to put me down, but they haven't succeeded, and they can't do it. (Interview of Joseph Smith, Nauvoo, Illinois, 21 Aug. 1843; in David Nye White, *Pittsburgh Weekly Gazette*, 15 Sept. 1843, [3].)

A Single-Narrative Harmony of the Accounts

A history of the life of Joseph Smith Jr.; an account of his marvelous experience and of all the mighty acts which he doeth in the name of Jesus Christ, the son of the living God, of whom he beareth record.

The Lord does reveal himself to me. I know it. He revealed himself first to me when I was about fourteen years old, a mere boy. I will tell you about when I received this first communication.

Owing to the many reports which have been put in circulation by evil-disposed and designing persons, in relation to the rise and progress of The Church of Jesus Christ of Latter-day Saints, all of which have been designed by the authors thereof to militate against its character as a Church and its progress in the world— I have been induced to write this history, to disabuse the public mind, and put all inquirers after truth in possession of the facts, as they have transpired, in relation both to myself and the Church, so far as I have such facts in my possession.

In this history I shall present the various events in relation to this Church, in truth and righteousness, as they have transpired, or as they at present exist, being now [1838] the eighth year since the organization of the said Church.

I was born in the year of our Lord one thousand eight hundred and five, on the twenty-third day of December, in the town of Sharon, Windsor county, State of Vermont, of goodly parents who spared no pains to instruct me in the Christian religion. My father, Joseph Smith, Sen., left the State of Vermont, and moved to Palmyra, Ontario (now Wayne) county, in the State of New York, when I was in my tenth year, or thereabouts. In about four years after my father's arrival in Palmyra, he moved with his family into Manchester in the same county of Ontario—

His family consisting of eleven souls, namely, my father, Joseph Smith; my mother, Lucy Smith (whose name, previous to her marriage, was Mack, daughter of Solomon Mack); my brothers, Alvin (who died November 19th, 1823, in the 26th year of his age), Hyrum, myself, Samuel Harrison, William, Don Carlos; and my sisters, Sophronia, Catherine, and Lucy.

And being in indigent circumstances, they were obliged to labor hard for the support of a large family, having nine children. And as it required the exertions of all that were able to render any assistance for the support of the family, therefore we were deprived of the benefit of an education. Suffice it to say I was merely instructed in reading, writing, and the ground rules of arithmetic, which constituted my whole literary acquirements.

My father was a farmer and taught me the art of husbandry.

At about the age of twelve years, my mind become seriously impressed with regard to the all-important concerns for the welfare of my immortal soul, which led me to searching the scriptures—believing, as I was taught, that they contained the word of God and thus applying myself to them.

When about fourteen years of age, I began to reflect upon the importance of being prepared for a future state, and upon enquiring about the plan of salvation, I found that there was a great clash in religious sentiment; if I went to one society, they referred me to one plan, and another to another, each one pointing to his own particular creed as the summum bonum of perfection.

My intimate acquaintance with those of different denominations led me to marvel exceedingly, for I discovered that they did not adorn their profession by a holy walk and godly conversation agreeable to what I found contained in that sacred depository. This was a grief to my soul.

Being wrought up in my mind respecting the subject of religion, and looking at the different systems taught the children of men, I knew not who was right or who was wrong but considered it of the first importance to me that I should be right in matters of so much moment, matter involving eternal consequences.

Thus, from the age of twelve years to fifteen I pondered many things in my heart concerning the situation of the world of mankind, the contentions and divisions, the wickedness and abominations, and the darkness which pervaded the minds of mankind. My mind became exceedingly distressed, for I became convicted of my sins, and by searching the scriptures I found that mankind did not come unto the Lord but that they had apostatized from the true and living faith, and there was no society or denomination that was built upon the gospel of Jesus Christ as recorded in the New Testament. I felt to mourn for my own sins and for the sins of the world, for I learned in the scriptures that God was the same yesterday, today, and forever, that he was no respecter of persons, for he was God.

For I looked upon the sun, the glorious luminary of the earth, and also the moon, rolling in their majesty through the heavens, and also the stars shining in their courses, and the earth also upon which I stood, and the beasts of the field, and the fowls of heaven, and the fish of the waters, and also man walking forth upon the face of the earth in majesty and in the strength of beauty, whose power and intelligence in governing the things which are so exceedingly great and marvelous, even in the likeness of him who created them.

And when I considered upon these things, my heart exclaimed, "Well hath the wise man said, 'It is a fool that saith in his heart, there is no God.'" My heart exclaimed, "All, all these bear testimony and bespeak an omnipotent and omnipresent power, a being who maketh laws and decreeth and bindeth all things in their bounds, who filleth eternity, who was and is and will be from all eternity to eternity." And I considered all these things and that that being seeketh such to worship him as worship him in spirit and in truth.

Some time in the second year after our removal to Manchester, there was in the place where we lived an unusual excitement on the subject of religion—a reformation among the different religious denominations in the neighborhood where I lived. It commenced with the Methodists, but soon became general among all the sects in that region of country. Indeed, the whole district of country seemed affected by it, and great multitudes united themselves to the different religious parties, which created no small stir and division amongst the people, some crying, "Lo, here!" and others, "Lo, there!" Some were contending for the Methodist faith, some for the Presbyterian, and some for the Baptist.

For, notwithstanding the great love which the converts to

these different faiths expressed at the time of their conversion, and the great zeal manifested by the respective clergy, who were active in getting up and promoting this extraordinary scene of religious feeling, in order to have everybody converted, as they were pleased to call it, let them join what sect they pleased; yet when the converts began to file off, some to one party and some to another, it was seen that the seemingly good feelings of both the priests and the converts were more pretended than real; for a scene of great confusion and bad feeling ensued—priest contending against priest, and convert against convert; so that all their good feelings one for another, if they ever had any, were entirely lost in a strife of words and a contest about opinions.

I was at this time in my fifteenth year. My father's family was proselyted to the Presbyterian faith, and four of them joined that church, namely, my mother, Lucy; my brothers Hyrum and Samuel Harrison; and my sister Sophronia.

During this time of great excitement my mind was called up to serious reflection and great uneasiness; but though my feelings were deep and often poignant, still I kept myself aloof from all these parties, though I attended their several meetings as often as occasion would permit. In process of time my mind became somewhat partial to the Methodist sect, and I felt some desire to be united with them; but so great were the confusion and strife among the different denominations, that it was impossible for a person young as I was, and so unacquainted with men and things, to come to any certain conclusion who was right and who was wrong.

My mind at times was greatly excited, the cry and tumult were so great and incessant. The Presbyterians were most decided against the Baptists and Methodists, and used all the powers of both reason and sophistry to prove their errors, or, at least, to make the people think they were in error. On the other hand, the Baptists and Methodists in their turn were equally zealous in endeavoring to establish their own tenets and disprove all others.

In the midst of this war of words and tumult of opinions, I often said to myself: What is to be done? Who of all these parties are right; or, are they all wrong together?[1] If any one of them be right, which is it, and how shall I know it? I became serious, and was desirous to know what Church to join.

Considering that all could not be right, and that God could not be the author of so much confusion, I determined to investigate the subject more fully, believing that if God had a church it would not be split up into factions, and that if he taught one society to worship one way, and administer in one set of ordinances, he would not teach another principles which were diametrically opposed.

While I was laboring under the extreme difficulties caused by the contests of these parties of religionists, While thinking of this matter, I was one day reading the Epistle of James,[2] first chapter and fifth verse, which reads: *If any of you lack wisdom, let him ask of God, that giveth to all men liberally, and upbraideth not; and it shall be given him.*

Believing the word of God, I had confidence in the declaration of James. Never did any passage of scripture come with more power to the heart of man than this did at this time to mine. It seemed to enter with great force into every feeling of my heart. I reflected on it again and again, knowing that if any person needed wisdom from God, I did; for how to act I did not know, and unless I could get more wisdom than I then had, I would never know; for the teachers of religion of the different sects understood the same passages of scripture so differently as to destroy all confidence in settling the question by an appeal to the Bible.

---

[1] This statement is from the 1838 reminiscence. Later in the same account, Joseph said, "My object in going to inquire of the Lord was to know which of all the sects was right . . . (for at this time it had never entered into my heart that all were wrong." The first statement seems to be in reference to the Presbyterians, Baptists, and Methodists, of whom Joseph wonders, "Who of all these parties are right; or, all they all wrong together?" The latter statement refers to "all the sects," a far broader category than the first.

[2] The David Nye White account says, "I opened the Testament promiscuously on these words . . ."

At length I came to the conclusion that I must either remain in darkness and confusion, or else I must do as James directs, that is, ask of God. I at length came to the determination to "ask of God," concluding that if he gave wisdom to them that lacked wisdom, and would give liberally, and not upbraid, I might venture.

And considering it of the first importance that I should be right in matters that involve eternal consequences, being thus perplexed in mind . . . , under a realizing sense that he had said (if the Bible be true), "Ask, and you shall receive; knock, and it shall be opened; seek, and you shall find," and again, "If any man lack wisdom, let him ask of God, who giveth to all men liberally, and upbraideth not."

So, in accordance with this, my determination to ask of God, I retired to the woods to make the attempt. It was on the morning of a beautiful, clear day, early in the spring of eighteen hundred and twenty. It was the first time in my life that I had made such an attempt, for amidst all my anxieties I had never as yet made the attempt to pray vocally.

After I had retired to the place where I had previously designed to go, a secret place in the silent grove where my father had a clearing, and went to the stump where I had stuck my axe when I had quit work, and having looked around me, and finding myself alone, I bowed down before the Lord, and began to call upon the Lord[,] offer[ing] up the desires of my heart to God.

Information was what I most desired at this time, and with a fixed determination to obtain it, I called upon the Lord for the first time in the place above stated.

I had scarcely done so, when immediately I was seized upon by some power which entirely overcame me, and had such an astonishing influence over me as to bind my tongue so that I could not speak.

Or in other words, I made a fruitless attempt to pray; my tongue seemed to be swollen in my mouth, so that I could not utter. I heard a noise behind me, like some person walking towards me. I strove again to pray but could not. The noise of walking seemed to draw nearer. I sprung up on my feet and looked

around but saw no person or thing that was calculated to produce the noise of walking.

I kneeled again. Thick darkness gathered around me, and it
seemed to me for a time as if I were doomed to sudden destruction.

But exerting all my powers to call upon God to deliver me out
of the power of this enemy which had seized upon me, and at the
very moment when I was ready to sink into despair and abandon
myself to destruction—not to an imaginary ruin, but to the power
of some actual being from the unseen world, who had such marvelous power as I had never before felt in any being—just at this
moment of great alarm,

My mouth was opened and my tongue liberated, and I called
on the Lord in mighty prayer[.] I saw a pillar of brilliant light
[and] fire exactly over my head, above the brightness of the sun
at noonday, which descended gradually from above until it fell
upon me and rested upon me.

It no sooner appeared than I found myself delivered from the
enemy which held me bound.

The Lord heard my cry in the wilderness, and I was filled with
the spirit of God and with joy unspeakable, and the Lord opened
the heavens upon me and I saw the Lord.

While fervently engaged in supplication, my mind was taken
away from the objects with which I was surrounded, and I was
enwrapped in a heavenly vision.

A glorious personage appeared in the midst of this pillar of
flame, which was spread all around and yet nothing consumed.
Another personage soon appeared, like unto the first—two glorious personages who exactly resembled each other in features
and likeness, whose brightness and glory defy all description,
standing above me in the air. One of them spake unto me, calling
me by name and said, pointing to the other—*This is My Beloved
Son. Hear Him!* He testified unto me that Jesus Christ is the son
of God.

My object in going to inquire of the Lord was to know which
of all the sects was right, that I might know which to join. No
sooner, therefore, did I get possession of myself, so as to be able

to speak, than I asked the Personages who stood above me in the light, which of all the sects was right (for at this time it had never entered into my heart that all were wrong). [And] I cried unto the Lord for mercy, for there was none else to whom I could go and obtain mercy.

I then addressed this second person, saying, "O Lord, what church shall I join?"

I was answered that I must join none of them, for they were all wrong; that all religious denominations were believing in incorrect doctrines and the Personage who addressed me said that all their creeds were an abomination in his sight; that those professors were all corrupt; that none of them was acknowledged of God as his church and kingdom. And I was expressly commanded to "go not after them," at the same time receiving a promise that the fulness of the gospel should at some future time be made known unto me.

And he spake unto me, saying, "Joseph, my son, thy sins are forgiven thee. Go thy way, walk in my statutes, and keep my commandments. Behold, I am the Lord of glory. I was crucified for the world, that all those who believe on my name may have eternal life. Behold, the world lieth in sin at this time, and none doeth good, no, not one. They have turned aside from the gospel and keep not my commandments. "They draw near to me with their lips, but their hearts are far from me, they teach for doctrines the commandments of men, having a form of godliness, but they deny the power thereof." And mine anger is kindling against the inhabitants of the earth, to visit them according to their ungodliness and to bring to pass that which hath been spoken by the mouth of the prophets and apostles. Behold and lo, I come quickly, as it is written of me, in the cloud, clothed in the glory of my Father."

He again forbade me to join with any of them; and many other things did he say unto me, which I cannot write at this time.

And I saw many angels in this vision.

The vision then vanished, and when I come to myself, I was sprawling on my back; looking up into heaven. When the light had departed, I had no strength[,] and it was some time before my strength returned; but soon recovering in some degree, I went home. And as I leaned up to the fireplace, mother inquired what the matter was. I replied, "Never mind, all is well—I am well enough off." I then said to my mother, "I have learned for myself that Presbyterianism is not true."

My soul was filled with love, and for many days I could rejoice with great joy. The Lord was with me, but I could find none that would believe the heavenly vision.

When I went home and told the people that I had a revelation, and that all the churches were corrupt, they persecuted me, and they have persecuted me ever since.

Nevertheless, I pondered these things in my heart.

It seems as though the adversary was aware, at a very early period of my life, that I was destined to prove a disturber and an annoyer of his kingdom; else why should the powers of darkness combine against me? Why the opposition and persecution that arose against me, almost in my infancy?

Some few days after I had this vision, I happened to be in company with one of the Methodist preachers, who was very active in the before mentioned religious excitement; and, conversing with him on the subject of religion, I took occasion to give him an account of the vision which I had had. I was greatly surprised at his behavior; he treated my communication not only lightly, but with great contempt, saying it was all of the devil, that there were no such things as visions or revelations in these days; that all such things had ceased with the apostles, and that there would never be any more of them.

I soon found, however, that my telling the story had excited a great deal of prejudice against me among professors of religion, and was the cause of great persecution, which continued to increase; and though I was an obscure boy, only between fourteen and fifteen years of age, and my circumstances in life such as to make a boy of no consequence in the world, yet men of high standing would take notice sufficient to excite the public mind against me, and create a bitter persecution; and this was common among all the sects—all united to persecute me.

It caused me serious reflection then, and often has since, how very strange it was that an obscure boy, of a little over fourteen years of age, and one, too, who was doomed to the necessity of obtaining a scanty maintenance by his daily labor, should be thought a character of sufficient importance to attract the attention of the great ones of the most popular sects of the day, and in a manner to create in them a spirit of the most bitter persecution and reviling. But strange or not, so it was, and it was often the cause of great sorrow to myself.

However, it was nevertheless a fact that I had beheld a vision. I have thought since, that I felt much like Paul, when he made his defense before King Agrippa, and related the account of the vision he had when he saw a light, and heard a voice; but still there were but few who believed him; some said he was dishonest, others said he was mad; and he was ridiculed and reviled. But all this did not destroy the reality of his vision. He had seen a vision, he knew he had, and all the persecution under heaven could not make it otherwise; and though they should persecute him unto death, yet he knew, and would know to his latest breath, that he had both seen a light and heard a voice speaking unto him, and all the world could not make him think or believe otherwise.

So it was with me. I had actually seen a light, and in the midst of that light I saw two Personages, and they did in reality speak to me; and though I was hated and persecuted for saying that I had seen a vision, yet it was true; and while they were persecuting me, reviling me, and speaking all manner of evil against me falsely for so saying, I was led to say in my heart: Why persecute me for telling the truth? I have actually seen a vision; and who am I that I can withstand God, or why does the world think to make me deny what I have actually seen? For I had seen a vision; I knew it, and I knew that God knew it, and I could not deny it, neither dared I do it; at least I knew that by so doing I would offend God, and come under condemnation.

I had now got my mind satisfied so far as the sectarian world was concerned—that it was not my duty to join with any of them, but to continue as I was until further directed. I had found the testimony of James to be true—that a man who lacked wisdom might ask of God, and obtain, and not be upbraided.

The Single-Narrative Harmony with Different Accounts Distinguished by Typefaces

The following section gives the same single-narrative harmony as that found above, but the sources of the various parts of the story are set apart by different typefaces.

Here is a key to the accounts and their corresponding typefaces:

1832 version: *italic sans serif (Gill Sans MT)*

1835 version: `roman serif (Courier New)`

1838 version: roman serif (Palatino Linotype; italics in the original are in SMALL CAPS)

1842 version: *italic serif (Palatino Linotype)*

1843 version: roman sans serif (Gill Sans MT)

A history of the life of Joseph Smith Jr.; an account of his marvelous experience and of all the mighty acts which he doeth in the name of Jesus Christ, the son of the living God, of whom he beareth record.

The Lord does reveal himself to me. I know it. He revealed himself first to me when I was about fourteen years old, a mere boy. I will tell you about `when I received this first communication.`

Owing to the many reports which have been put in circulation by evil-disposed and designing persons, in relation to the rise and progress of The Church of Jesus Christ of Latter-day Saints, all of which have been designed by the authors thereof to militate against its character as a Church and its progress in the world— I have been induced to write this history, to disabuse the public mind, and put all inquirers after truth in possession of the facts, as they have transpired, in relation both to myself and the Church, so far as I have such facts in my possession.

In this history I shall present the various events in relation to this Church, in truth and righteousness, as they have transpired, or as they at present exist, being now [1838] the eighth year since the organization of the said Church.

I was born in the year of our Lord one thousand eight hundred and five, on the twenty-third day of December, in the town of Sharon, Windsor county, State of Vermont, *of goodly parents who spared no pains to instruct me in the Christian religion.* My father, Joseph Smith, Sen., left the State of Vermont, and moved to Palmyra, Ontario (now Wayne) county, in the State of New York, when I was in my tenth year, or thereabouts. In about four years after my father's arrival in Palmyra, he moved with his family into Manchester in the same county of Ontario—

His family consisting of eleven souls, namely, my father, Joseph Smith; my mother, Lucy Smith (whose name, previous to her marriage, was Mack, daughter of Solomon Mack); my brothers, Alvin (who died November 19th, 1823, in the 26th year of his age), Hyrum, myself, Samuel Harrison, William, Don Carlos; and my sisters, Sophronia, Catherine, and Lucy.

And being in indigent circumstances, they were obliged to labor hard for the support of a large family, having nine children. And as it required the exertions of all that were able to render any assistance for the support of the family, therefore we were deprived of the benefit of an education. Suffice it to say I was merely instructed in reading, writing, and the ground rules of arithmetic, which constituted my whole literary acquirements.

My father was a farmer and taught me the art of husbandry.

At about the age of twelve years, my mind become seriously impressed with regard to the all-important concerns for the welfare of my immortal soul, which led me to searching the scriptures—believing, as I was taught, that they contained the word of God and thus applying myself to them.

When about fourteen years of age, I began to reflect upon the importance of being prepared for a future state, and upon enquiring about the plan of salvation, I found that there was a great clash in religious sentiment; if I went to one society, they referred me to one plan, and another to another, each one pointing to his own particular creed as the summum bonum of perfection.

My intimate acquaintance with those of different denominations led me to marvel exceedingly, for I discovered that they did not adorn their profession by a holy walk and godly conversation agreeable to what I found contained in that sacred depository. This was a grief to my soul.

Being wrought up in my mind respecting the subject of Religion, and looking at the different systems taught the children of men, I knew not who was right

or who was wrong but considered it of the first importance to me that I should be right in matters of
so much moment, matter involving eternal consequences.

Thus, from the age of twelve years to fifteen I pondered many things in my heart concerning the situation of the world of mankind, the contentions and divisions, the wickedness and abominations, and the darkness which pervaded the minds of mankind. My mind became exceedingly distressed, for I became convicted of my sins, and by searching the scriptures I found that mankind did not come unto the Lord but that they had apostatized from the true and living faith, and there was no society or denomination that was built upon the gospel of Jesus Christ as recorded in the New Testament. I felt to mourn for my own sins and for the sins of the world, for I learned in the scriptures that God was the same yesterday, today, and forever, that he was no respecter of persons, for he was God.

For I looked upon the sun, the glorious luminary of the earth, and also the moon, rolling in their majesty through the heavens, and also the stars shining in their courses, and the earth also upon which I stood, and the beasts of the field, and the fowls of heaven, and the fish of the waters, and also man walking forth upon the face of the earth in majesty and in the strength of beauty, whose power and intelligence in governing the things which are so exceedingly great and marvelous, even in the likeness of him who created them. And when I considered upon these things, my heart exclaimed, "Well hath the wise man said, 'It is a fool that saith in his heart, there is no God.'" My heart exclaimed, "All, all these bear testimony and bespeak an omnipotent and omnipresent power, a being who maketh laws and decreeth and bindeth all things in their bounds, who filleth eternity, who was and is and will be from all eternity to eternity." And I considered all these things and that that being seeketh such to worship him as worship him in spirit and in truth.

Some time in the second year after our removal to Manchester, there was in the place where we lived an unusual excitement on the subject of religion — a reformation among the different religious denominations in the neighborhood where I lived. It commenced with the Methodists, but soon became general among all the sects in that region of country. Indeed, the whole district of country seemed affected by it, and great multitudes united themselves to the different religious parties, which created no small stir and division amongst the people, some crying, "Lo, here!" and others, "Lo, there!" Some were contending for the Methodist faith, some for the Presbyterian, and some for the Baptist.

For, notwithstanding the great love which the converts to these different faiths expressed at the time of their conversion, and the great zeal manifested by the respective clergy, who were active in getting up and promoting this extraordinary scene of religious feeling, in order to have everybody converted, as they were pleased to call it, let them join what sect they pleased; yet when the converts began to file off, some to one party and some to another, it was seen that the seemingly good feelings of both the priests and the converts were more pretended than real; for a scene of great confusion and bad feeling ensued—priest contending against priest, and convert against convert; so that all their good feelings one for another, if they ever had any, were entirely lost in a strife of words and a contest about opinions.

I was at this time in my fifteenth year. My father's family was proselyted to the Presbyterian faith, and four of them joined that church, namely, my mother, Lucy; my brothers Hyrum and Samuel Harrison; and my sister Sophronia.

During this time of great excitement my mind was called up to serious reflection and great uneasiness; but though my feelings were deep and often poignant, still I kept myself aloof from all these parties, though I attended their several meetings as often as occasion would permit. In process of time my mind became somewhat partial to the Methodist sect, and I felt some desire to be united with them; but so great were the confusion and strife among the different denominations, that it was impossible for a person young as I was, and so unacquainted with men and things, to come to any certain conclusion who was right and who was wrong.

My mind at times was greatly excited, the cry and tumult were so great and incessant. The Presbyterians were most decided against the Baptists and Methodists, and used all the powers of both reason and sophistry to prove their errors, or, at least, to make the people think they were in error. On the other hand, the Baptists and Methodists in their turn were equally zealous in endeavoring to establish their own tenets and disprove all others.

In the midst of this war of words and tumult of opinions, I often said to myself: What is to be done? Who of all these parties are right; or, are they all wrong together?[3] If any one of them be right, which is it, and how shall I know it? I became serious, and was desirous to know what Church to join.

Considering that all could not be right, and that God could not be the author of so much confusion, I determined to investigate the subject more fully, believing that if God had a church it would not be split up into factions, and that if he taught one society to worship one way, and administer in one set of ordinances, he would not teach another principles which were diametrically opposed.

While I was laboring under the extreme difficulties caused by the contests of these parties of religionists, While thinking of this matter, I was one day reading the Epistle of James,[4] first chapter and fifth verse, which reads: IF ANY OF YOU LACK WISDOM, LET HIM ASK OF GOD, THAT GIVETH TO ALL MEN LIBERALLY, AND UPBRAIDETH NOT; AND IT SHALL BE GIVEN HIM.

Believing the word of God, I had confidence in the declaration of James. Never did any passage of scripture come with more power to the heart of man than this did at this time to mine. It seemed to enter with great force into every feeling of my heart. I reflected on it again and again, knowing that if any person needed wisdom from God, I did; for how to act I did not know, and unless I could get more wisdom than I then had, I would never know; for the teachers of religion of the different sects understood the same passages of scripture so differently as to destroy all confidence in settling the question by an appeal to the Bible.

At length I came to the conclusion that I must either remain in darkness and confusion, or else I must do as James directs,

---

[3] This statement is from the 1838 reminiscence. Later in the same account, Joseph said, "My object in going to inquire of the Lord was to know which of all the sects was right . . . (for at this time it had never entered into my heart that all were wrong." The first statement seems to be in reference to the Presbyterians, Baptists, and Methodists, of whom Joseph wonders, "Who of *all these parties* are right; or, all they all wrong together?" The latter statement refers to "*all the sects*," a far broader category than the first.

[4] The David Nye White account says, "I opened the Testament promiscuously on these words. . . ."

that is, ask of God. I at length came to the determination to "ask of God," concluding that if he gave wisdom to them that lacked wisdom, and would give liberally, and not upbraid, I might venture.

And considering it of the first importance that I should be right in matters that involve eternal consequences, being thus perplexed in mind . . . , under a realizing sense that he had said (if the Bible be true), "Ask, and you shall receive; knock, and it shall be opened; seek, and you shall find," and again, "If any man lack wisdom, let him ask of God, who giveth to all men liberally, and upbraideth not."

So, in accordance with this, my determination to ask of God, I retired to the woods to make the attempt. It was on the morning of a beautiful, clear day, early in the spring of eighteen hundred and twenty. It was the first time in my life that I had made such an attempt, for amidst all my anxieties I had never as yet made the attempt to pray vocally.

After I had retired to the place where I had previously designed to go, *a secret place in* the silent grove where my father had a clearing, and went to the stump where I had stuck my axe when I had quit work, and having looked around me, and finding myself alone, I bowed down before the Lord, and began *to call upon the Lord[,]* offer[ing] up the desires of my heart to God.

Information was what I most desired at this time, and with a fixed determination to obtain it, I called upon the Lord for the first time in the place above stated.

I had scarcely done so, when immediately I was seized upon by some power which entirely overcame me, and had such an astonishing influence over me as to bind my tongue so that I could not speak.

Or in other words, I made a fruitless attempt to pray; my tongue seemed to be swollen in my mouth, so that I could not utter. I heard a noise behind me, like some person walking towards me. I strove again to pray but could not. The noise of walking seemed to draw nearer. I sprung up on my feet and looked around but saw no person or thing that was calculated to produce the noise of walking.

I kneeled again. Thick darkness gathered around me, and it seemed to me for a time as if I were doomed to sudden destruction.

But exerting all my powers to call upon God to deliver me out of the power of this enemy which had seized upon me, and at the very moment when I was ready to sink into despair and abandon myself to destruction—not to an imaginary ruin, but to the power of some actual being from the unseen world, who had such marvelous power as I had never before felt in any being—just at this moment of great alarm,

My mouth was opened and my tongue liberated, and I called on the Lord in mighty prayer[.] I saw a pillar of *brilliant light [and] fire* exactly over my head, above the brightness of the sun *at noonday,* which descended gradually **from above** until it fell upon me *and rested upon me.*

It no sooner appeared than I found myself delivered from the enemy which held me bound.

The Lord heard my cry in the wilderness, and I was filled with the spirit of God and with joy unspeakable, *and the Lord opened the heavens upon me and I saw the Lord.*

While fervently engaged in supplication, my mind was taken away from the objects with which I was surrounded, and I was enwrapped in a heavenly vision.

A **glorious** personage appeared in the midst of this pillar of flame, which was spread all around and yet nothing consumed. Another personage soon appeared, like unto the first—*two glorious personages who exactly resembled each other in features and likeness,* whose brightness and glory defy all description, standing above me in the air. One of them spake unto me, calling me by name and said, pointing to the other—THIS IS MY BELOVED SON. HEAR HIM! He testified unto me that Jesus Christ is the son of God.

My object in going to inquire of the Lord was to know which of all the sects was right, that I might know which to join. No sooner, therefore, did I get possession of myself, so as to be able to speak, than I asked the Personages who stood above me in the light, which of all the sects was right (for at this time it had never entered into my heart that all were wrong). *[And] I cried unto the Lord for mercy, for there was none else to whom I could go and obtain mercy.*

I then addressed this second person, saying, "O Lord, what church shall I join?"

I was answered that I must join none of them, for they were all wrong; *that all religious denominations were believing in incorrect doctrines* and the Personage who addressed me said that all their creeds were an abomination in his sight; that those professors were all corrupt; *that none of them was acknowledged of God as his church and kingdom. And I was expressly commanded to "go not after them," at the same time receiving a promise that the fulness of the gospel should at some future time be made known unto me.*

And he spake unto me, saying, "Joseph, my son, thy sins are forgiven thee. Go thy way, walk in my statutes, and keep my commandments. Behold, I am the Lord of glory. I was crucified for the world, that all those who believe on my name may have eternal life. Behold, the world lieth in sin at this time, and none doeth good, no, not one. They have turned aside from the gospel and keep not my commandments. "They draw near to me with their lips, but their hearts are far from me, they teach for doctrines the commandments of men, having a form of godliness, but they deny the power thereof." *And mine anger is kindling against the inhabitants of the earth, to visit them according to their ungodliness and to bring to pass that which hath been spoken by the mouth of the prophets and apostles. Behold and lo, I come quickly, as it is written of me, in the cloud, clothed in the glory of my Father."*

He again forbade me to join with any of them; and many other things did he say unto me, which I cannot write at this time.

`And I saw many angels in this vision.`

The vision then vanished, and when I come to myself, I was sprawling on my back; looking up into heaven. When the light had departed, I had no strength[,] and it was some time before my strength returned; but soon recovering in some degree, I went home. And as I leaned up to the fireplace, mother inquired what the matter was. I replied, "Never mind, all is well—I am well enough off." I then said to my mother, "I have learned for myself that Presbyterianism is not true."

My soul was filled with love, and for many days I could rejoice with great joy. The Lord was with me, but I could find none that would believe the heavenly vision.

When I went home and told the people that I had a revelation, and that all the churches were corrupt, they persecuted me, and they have persecuted me ever since.

Nevertheless, I pondered these things in my heart.

It seems as though the adversary was aware, at a very early period of my life, that I was destined to prove a disturber and an annoyer of his kingdom; else why should the powers of darkness combine against me? Why the opposition and persecution that arose against me, almost in my infancy?

Some few days after I had this vision, I happened to be in company with one of the Methodist preachers, who was very active in the before mentioned religious excitement; and, conversing with him on the subject of religion, I took occasion to give him an account of the vision which I had had. I was greatly surprised at his behavior; he treated my communication not only lightly, but with great contempt, saying it was all of the devil, that there were no such things as visions or revelations in these days; that all such things had ceased with the apostles, and that there would never be any more of them.

I soon found, however, that my telling the story had excited a great deal of prejudice against me among professors of religion, and was the cause of great persecution, which continued to increase; and though I was an obscure boy, only between fourteen and fifteen years of age, and my circumstances in life such as to make a boy of no consequence in the world, yet men of high standing would take notice sufficient to excite the public mind against me, and create a bitter persecution; and this was common among all the sects—all united to persecute me.

It caused me serious reflection then, and often has since, how very strange it was that an obscure boy, of a little over fourteen years of age, and one, too, who was doomed to the necessity of obtaining a scanty maintenance by his daily labor, should be thought a character of sufficient importance to attract the attention of the great ones of the most popular sects of the day, and in a manner to create in them a spirit of the most bitter persecution and reviling. But strange or not, so it was, and it was often the cause of great sorrow to myself.

However, it was nevertheless a fact that I had beheld a vision.

I have thought since, that I felt much like Paul, when he made his defense before King Agrippa, and related the account of the vision he had when he saw a light, and heard a voice; but still there were but few who believed him; some said he was dishonest, others said he was mad; and he was ridiculed and reviled. But all this did not destroy the reality of his vision. He had seen a vision, he knew he had, and all the persecution under heaven could not make it otherwise; and though they should persecute him unto death, yet he knew, and would know to his latest breath, that he had both seen a light and heard a voice speaking unto him, and all the world could not make him think or believe otherwise.

So it was with me. I had actually seen a light, and in the midst of that light I saw two Personages, and they did in reality speak to me; and though I was hated and persecuted for saying that I had seen a vision, yet it was true; and while they were persecuting me, reviling me, and speaking all manner of evil against me falsely for so saying, I was led to say in my heart: Why persecute me for telling the truth? I have actually seen a vision; and who am I that I can withstand God, or why does the world think to make me deny what I have actually seen? For I had seen a vision; I knew it, and I knew that God knew it, and I could not deny it, neither dared I do it; at least I knew that by so doing I would offend God, and come under condemnation.

I had now got my mind satisfied so far as the sectarian world was concerned—that it was not my duty to join with any of them, but to continue as I was until further directed. I had found the testimony of James to be true—that a man who lacked wisdom might ask of God, and obtain, and not be upbraided.

Part 2

Some critics find fault with the fact that we don't have more contemporary accounts of Joseph Smith's vision. But Elder Richard J. Maynes of the presidency of the Seventy has a different view. He observed that Joseph Smith gave us four accounts of the First Vision and his contemporaries provided five more. "It is a blessing to have these records," he said. They make Joseph's First Vision the best-documented vision in history." (*Ensign,* June 2017, 62.)

This is a significant insight. Consider the great visions and visitations found in the scriptures—God walking with Adam and Eve in the Garden of Eden; Abraham entertaining angels in his tent; Moses conversing with God on the mount; Peter, James, and John seeing the transfiguration of Jesus—and his visit with Moses and Elijah—and many more. We have limited witnesses of these amazing experiences. Yet each person can know of their truthfulness through the Holy Ghost.

Latter-day Saints likewise know of the reality of Joseph Smith's First Vision through the Holy Ghost. It is wonderful to know that there were people who knew Joseph Smith personally, who heard him tell of his vision, who believed him, and who made a record of what they learned. This section brings together four accounts of people who heard Joseph's story from his own mouth and recorded their experience while Joseph was still alive: Orson Pratt, Orson Hyde, Levi Richards, and Alexander Neibaur.

Even with these accounts, some may wonder why there are not even more. Scholar Hugh Nibley gives us a possible explanation. His great-grandfather, Nibley said, was a Jew named Alexander Neibaur. "One day after he had given Joseph Smith a lesson in German and Hebrew [he] asked him about certain particulars of the first vision. In reply he was told some remarkable things, which he wrote down in his journal that very day. But in the ensuing forty years of his life . . . Brother Neibaur seems never once to have referred to the wonderful things the Prophet told him—it was quite by accident that the writer [Nibley] discovered them in his journal. Why was the talkative old man so close-lipped on the one thing that could have made him famous? Because it was a sacred and privileged communication; it was never published to the world and never should be." (*Improvement Era*, July 1961, 522.)

So it may have been with others who heard a retelling of that marvelous vision directly from the lips of the man who had experienced it. They may have been reticent to say much publicly because "it was a sacred and privileged communication."

Even if some (or many) who personally heard Joseph Smith's testimony initially held it close, in time they began to share what they had learned. History gives many accounts from people who knew Joseph well, heard him tell the story of the First Vision, and then recorded or recounted it later. These include such apostolic associates as Brigham Young, John Taylor, Wilford Woodruff, Lorenzo Snow, William Smith, Parley P. Pratt, Orson Pratt (who told the story repeatedly), and George A. Smith; George Q. Cannon (who became an apostle later); and several less prominent but believing Church members: Edward Stevenson, Mary Isabella Hales Horne, John Alger, and Milo Andrus.

Truly, the First Vision is "the best-documented vision in history."

Elder Maynes continued, "Like the individual New Testament

Gospels that together more completely describe Christ's life and ministry, each one of the accounts describing Joseph's First Vision adds unique detail and perspective to the total experience. They together tell Joseph's consistent, harmonious story." (*Ensign,* June 2017, 63.) The accounts have important common elements: that different preachers were teaching contradictory doctrines, that Joseph was eager to know the truth, that he searched the scriptures for an answer and then was motivated to pray, that he saw a glorious light, and that heavenly beings appeared in the grove and gave him the answer he sought.

These common elements are found in the accounts gathered in this section of the book. Included are witnesses who were close associates of Joseph Smith: his brother William; his cousin George A. Smith; his Hebrew teacher Alexander Neibaur; and apostles Brigham Young, Parley P. Pratt, Orson Pratt, Orson Hyde, John Taylor, Wilford Woodruff, and Lorenzo Snow. Also found in this section are others who appear to have had less contact with Joseph but who heard his story and believed with all their hearts.

The accounts recorded or reported by Joseph's contemporaries are arranged in rough chronological order. First are the accounts that were written before the martyrdom of the Prophet, as well as those that were recorded later but can be tied to a specific year of the prophet's life. Then we present those that were written or spoken after his death. Where the record provides more than one retelling from a given individual, those accounts are grouped and arranged in chronological order before the accounts from the next person are given. As needed, these accounts are presented with spelling and punctuation standardized. In some cases, to increase readability, paragraph breaks have been introduced. To reduce the inevitable repetition, in some instances only a portion of a particular account is included.

William Smith

William Smith (1811–1893) was a younger brother of Joseph Smith. He was called as an apostle in 1835. Note that in his old-age reminiscences, William Smith often conflated some of the events of First Vision with those attending the visits of the angel Moroni.

It will be remembered that just before the angel appeared to Joseph, there was an unusual revival in the neighborhood. It spread from town to town, from city to city, from county to county, and from state to state. My mother attended those meetings, and being much concerned about the spiritual welfare of the family, she persuaded them to attend the meetings. Finally my mother, one sister, my brothers Samuel, and Hyrum became Presbyterians. Joseph and myself did not join; I had not sown all my wild oats. At the close of these meetings the different ministers began to beat around to see how many converts they could get to join their respective churches. All said, Come and join us, we are right. Where is the gospel of Christ? Where is the church of Christ? There is a lost gospel. There is a lost church.

And here let me say, that it was at the suggestion of the Rev. M____, that my brother asked of God. He said, "Ask of God." It was the church of Christ he was seeking for, what all should seek. God promised to give knowledge to all who lacked, if they would ask.

Accordingly he went and bowed in prayer, he saw a pillar of fire descending. Saw it reach the top of the trees. He was overcome, became unconscious, did not know how long he remained in this condition, but when he came to himself, the great light was about him, and he was told by the personage whom he saw descend with the light, not to join any of the churches. That he should be instrumental in the hands of God in establishing the true church of Christ. (*Saints' Herald*, 4 Oct. 1884, 643.)

"Did you not doubt Joseph's testimony sometimes?" asked Brother Briggs.

"No," was the reply by William Smith. "We all had the most implicit confidence in what he said. He was a truthful boy. Father and mother believed him, why should not the children? I suppose if he had told crooked stories about other things we might have doubted his word about the plates, but Joseph was a truthful boy. That father and mother believed his report and suffered persecution for that belief shows that he was truthful. No, sir, we never doubted his word for one minute."

"Were your folks religiously inclined before Joseph saw the angel?" asked Brother Briggs.

"Yes, we always had family prayers since I can remember.

"Hyrum, Samuel, Katherine, and Mother were members of the Presbyterian Church. My father would not join. He did not like it because a Rev. Stockton had preached my brother's funeral sermon and intimated very strongly that he had gone to hell, for Alvin was not a church member, but he was a good boy, and my father did not like it."

"What caused Joseph to ask for guidance as to what church he ought to join?" asked Brother Briggs.

"Why, there was a joint revival," was the reply, "in the neighborhood between the Baptists, Methodists, and Presbyterians, and they had succeeded in stirring up quite a feeling and after the meeting the question arose which church should have the converts. Rev. Stockton was the president of the meeting and suggested that it was their meeting and under their care, and they had a church there and they ought to join the Presbyterians, but as father did not like Rev. Stockton very well, our folks hesitated, and the next evening a Rev. Mr. Lane of the Methodists preached a sermon on `what church shall I join?' and the burden of his discourse was to ask God, using as a text, `If any man lack wisdom let him ask of God, who giveth to all men liberally.'

"And of course when Joseph went home and was looking over the text, he was impressed to do just what the preacher had said, and going out in the woods with child-like, simple trusting faith, believing that God meant just what He said, he kneeled down and prayed; and the time having come for the reorganization of His Church, God was pleased to show him that he should join none of these churches, but if faithful he should be chosen to establish the true Church." (*Millennial Star*, 26 Feb. 1894, 133–134.)

Lorenzo Snow

Lorenzo Snow (1814–1901) first heard Joseph's testimony in about 1832. He was called to be an apostle in 1849 and as Church president in 1898.

When about 15 years of age, being seriously impressed with the necessity of seeking the Lord and preparing for a future state, [Joseph's] mind became much perplexed through difficulties thrown in the path of his researches by the multitude of religious sects and parties with which he was surrounded. Each system claimed its right and power to give belief and hope, but none to communicate knowledge of its divine authority. In comparing them one with another there seemed too much confusion, the same also appeared in looking at each separately: —turning therefore from these clashing systems, and having been encouraged, and inspired with the following passage in St. James: "If any of you lack wisdom let him ask of God;" he retired to a grove, a little distance from his father's, and in fervent prayer besought the Lord to communicate with him, and reveal the way of salvation.

While thus engaged a light brilliant and glorious appeared in the heavens gradually descending towards him till he was enveloped in its power, and wrapped in celestial vision; when he beheld two glorious beings similar in dress and appearance who informed him that the religious sects had all departed from the ancient doctrine of the apostles, and that the Gospel, with its gifts and blessings should be made known to him at a future period. Many important things were manifested in this vision which the brevity of this work will not admit our noticing. (Snow, *The Voice of Joseph* [1852], 3.)

We testify to the whole world that we know, by divine revelation, even through the manifestations of the Holy Ghost, that Jesus is the Christ, the Son of the living God, and that He revealed Himself to Joseph Smith as personally as He did to His Apostles, anciently, after He arose from the tomb, and that He made known unto him those heavenly truths by which alone mankind can be saved. (*Journal of Discourses*, 18:298.)

Over sixty years ago I saw for the first time Joseph Smith, the Prophet of the Lord. He was holding a meeting in the town of Hiram. He was about three miles from where I was born and brought up. He was standing by a door and talking to an audience of about 250 persons under a bowery. I was about eighteen years of age. I had heard something about the "Mormon" Prophet, I felt some anxiety to see him and judge for myself, as he was generally believed to be a false prophet. My mother and my two sisters (one of whom was Eliza R. Snow) received the principles of "Mormonism" and were baptized.

At the time I refer to, Joseph Smith was not what would be called a fluent speaker. He simply bore his testimony to what the Lord had manifested to him, to the dispensation of the Gospel which had been committed to him, and to the authority that he possessed. As I looked upon him and listened, I thought to myself that a man bearing such a wonderful testimony as he did, and having such a countenance as he possessed, could hardly be a false prophet. He certainly could not have been deceived, it seemed to me, and if he was a deceiver he was deceiving the people knowingly; for when he testified that he had had a conversation with Jesus, the Son of God, and had talked with Him personally, as Moses is said to have talked with God upon Mount Sinai, and that he had also heard the voice of the Father, he was telling something that he either knew to be false or positively true. (*Deseret Evening News*, 20 July 1901, 22.)

Milo Andrus

Milo Andrus (1814–1893) joined the Church in 1832 but didn't hear Joseph's testimony until a year later. He shared his memory of that experience in 1853. Andrus later became a bishop, stake president, and patriarch. He led three pioneer groups to Utah.

I was a boy first 19 years of age when I heard the testimony of that man Joseph Smith that angel came and that [glory?] and trees seemed to be consumed in blaze and he was there entrusted with this information that darkness covered the earth that the great mass of Christian world universally wrong their creeds all upon uncertain foundation now as young as you are I call upon you from this obscurity go forth and build up my kingdom on the earth. (Speech, 17 July 1853, Salt Lake City; in Papers of George D. Watt, MS 4534, box 2, disk 1, May 1853–July 1853, images 231–256, LDS Church History Library. Transcribed by LaJean Purcell Carruth, 3 Oct. 2012; corrected Oct. 2013.)

Edward Stevenson

Edward Stevenson (1820–1897) was born in Spain only weeks after Joseph Smith experienced his First Vision. Stevenson first heard Joseph's testimony in 1834. He later went on six missions, led two pioneer groups to Utah, and served as one of the seven presidents of the Seventy.

In that same year, 1834, in the midst of many large congregations the Prophet testified with great power concerning the visit of the Father and the Son, and the conversation he had with them. Never before did I feel such power as was manifested on these occasions. . . .

Although a mere widow's son, I felt proud and blessed of God, when he honored us by coming under our roof and

partaking of our hospitality. . . . We were proud, indeed, to en-
tertain one who had conversed with the Father and the Son, and
been under the tuition of an angel from heaven. (Stevenson, *Reminiscences of Joseph, the Prophet* [1893], 4–5.)

It was on those school grounds where two Mormon Elders introduced the restored gospel in the year 1833; and in 1834 Joseph
Smith the Prophet preached with such power as had not there
ever before been witnessed in this nineteenth century. . . . I can
very well remember many of the words of the boy Prophet as
they were uttered in simplicity, but with a power which was
irresistible to all present. . . . With uplifted hand he said: "I am a
witness that there is a God, for I saw Him in open day, while
praying in a silent grove, in the spring of 1820." He further testified that God, the Eternal Father, pointing to a separate personage, in the likeness of Himself, said: "This is my Beloved Son,
hear ye Him." Oh, how these words thrilled my entire system,
and filled me with joy unspeakable to behold one who, like Paul
the apostle of olden time, could with boldness testify that he had
been in the presence of Jesus Christ! (*Juvenile Instructor*, 15 July
1894, 444–445.)

A great stir was made in this settlement [Pontiac, Michigan] at
so distinguished visitors the meetings held were crowded to see
and hear the testimonies given which were very powerful I will
here relate my own experience on the occasion of a meeting in
our old log school House The Prophet stood at a table for the pul-
pit where he began relating his vision and before he got through
he was in the midst of the congregation with uplifted hand. I do
believe that there was not one person present who did at the time
being or who was not convicted of the truth of his vision, of an
Angle to him his countenance seemed to me to assume a heavenly whiteness and his voice was so piercing and forcible for my
part it so impressed me as to become indelibly imprinted in my
mind. ("The Life and History of Elder Edward Stevenson," 21,
LDS Church History Library.)

Parley P. Pratt

Parley P. Pratt (1807–1857) was called to be an apostle in 1835. In 1836 he recorded that he heard Joseph Smith bear a powerful testimony of the First Vision. He was an older brother of Orson Pratt, listed below.

One week before word was publicly given that Br. J. Smith Jr. would give a relation of the coming forth of the records and also of the rise of the church and of his experience. Accordingly a vast concourse assembled at an early hour. Every seat was crowded and 4 or 5 hundred People stood up in the Aisles. Br. S[mith] gave the history of these things relating many Particulars of the manner of his first visions &c. the Spirit and Power of God was upon him in Bearing testimony insomuch that many if not most of the congregation were in tears—as for my self I can say that all the reasonings in uncertainty and all the conclusions drawn from the writings of others . . . however great in themselves dwindle into insignificance when compared with the living testimony when your Eyes sea and your Ears hear from the living oracles of God. (Parley P. Pratt to the Elders and Brethren of the Church of Latter-day Saints in Canada, 27 Nov. 1836, LDS Church History Library.)

Joseph Curtis

Joseph Curtis (1818–1883) was baptized in 1833. He first heard Joseph bear testimony of the First Vision in 1835.

In the spring of 1835 [October 1834] Joseph Smith in Company with his father & mother & some others came to Michigan & paid us a visit—in a meeting stated the reason why he preached the doctrine he did I will state a few things according to my memory—as a revival of some of the sects was going on some of his father's family joined in with the revival himself being quite young he feeling anxiety to be religious his mind somewhat troubled this scripture came to his mind which says if a man lack wisdom let him ask of God who giveth liberally and upbraideth not believing it he went with a determination to obtain to enquire of the Lord himself after some struggle the Lord manifested to him that the different sects were wrong also that the Lord had a great work for him to do—it worried his mind—he told his father—his father told him to do as the Lord manifested—had other manifestations; saw an angel with a view of the hill Cumorah & the plates of gold had certain instructions got the plates & by the assistance of the Urim & Thummim translated them by the gift & power of God; also stated he done nothing except he more than he was commanded to do & for this his name was cast out as evil for this he was persecuted. ("Joseph Curtis reminiscence and diary, 1839 October–1881 March," MS 1654, pp. 5–6, LDS Church History Library.)

Mary Isabella Hales Horne

Mary Isabella Hales Horne (1818–1905) was baptized in 1836 and a year later heard Joseph speak of the First Vision with "wonderful power." She later served as president of the Salt Lake Stake Relief Society for twenty-six years.

I first met the Prophet Joseph Smith in the fall of 1837, at my home in the town of Scarborough, Canada West. When I first shook hands with him I was thrilled through and through and I knew that he was a Prophet of God. That testimony has never left me, but is still strong within me. . . .

The last time I shook hands with the Prophet was at the Mansion House, on an occasion when I had called to see part of the family.

I testify that Joseph Smith was the greatest Prophet that ever lived on this earth, the Savior, only, excepted. There was a personal magnetism about him which drew all people who became acquainted with him, to him.

I feel greatly honored when I realize that I have had the privilege of personally entertaining this great man, of ministering to his temporal wants, of shaking hands with him, and listening to his voice. I heard him relate his first vision when the Father and Son appeared to him; also his receiving the Gold Plates from the Angel Moroni. This recital was given in compliance with a special request of a few particular friends in the home of Sister Walton, whose house was ever open to the Saints. While he was relating the circumstances [of the First Vision], the Prophet's countenance lighted up, and so wonderful a power accompanied his words that everybody who heard them felt his influence and power, and none could doubt the truth of his narration. I know that he was true to his trust, and that the principles that he advanced and taught are true. (Testimony of Sister M. Isabella Horne, LDS Church History Library, quoted in *Young Woman's Journal*, Apr. 1920, 211–212.)

John Alger

John Alger (1820–1897), who was baptized in 1832, first heard Joseph's testimony in the early 1830s. Alger remembers a unique detail from that account and may have misremembered, either because he was very young when he heard the story or because he did not record it until sixty years later. Joseph Smith officiated at Alger's marriage in Nauvoo in 1842.

2nd Feb Thurs [1893] Cold and chilly. Attended Fast Meeting . . . Br John Alger said while speaking of the Prophet Joseph, that when he, John, was a small boy he heard the Prophet Joseph relate his vision of seeing The Father and the Son, That God touched his eyes with his finger and said "Joseph this is my beloved Son hear him." As soon as the Lord had touched his eyes with his finger he immediately saw the Savior.

After meeting, a few of us questioned him about the matter and he told us at the bottom of the meeting house steps that he was in the House of Father Smith in Kirtland when Joseph made this declaration, and that Joseph while speaking of it put his finger to his right eye, suiting the action with the words so as to illustrate and at the same time impress the occurrence on the minds of those unto whom he was speaking. We enjoyed the conversation very much, as it was something that we had never seen in church history or heard of before. (Charles Walker, diary, 2 Feb. 1893, in A. Karl Larsen and Katharine Miles Larsen, eds., *Diary of Charles Lowell Walker* [1980], 2:755–756.)

Levi Richards

Levi Richards (1799–1876) served as a physician for Joseph Smith and others in Nauvoo. He first heard Joseph's testimony in 1843. His younger brother was Willard Richards, an apostle. Willard was personal secretary to Joseph Smith and was present with the Prophet at the martyrdom.

Attended meeting at the temple weather very fine moderately warm. Heard J. Smith preach from Math [Matthew] "Oh Jerusalem Jerusalem &c, how oft would I have gathered you, as a hen gathereth her chickens under her wings & Ye would not, behold your house is left unto you desolate" &c.

Pres. J. Smith bore testimony to the same saying that when he was a youth he began to think about these things but could not find out which of all the sects were right he went into the grove & enquired of the Lord which of all the sects were right he received for answer that none of them were right, that they were all wrong, & that the everlasting covenant was broken—he said he understood the fulness of the gospel from beginning to end—& could teach it & also the order of the priesthood in all its ramifications—

Earth & hell had opposed him & tried to destroy him, but they had not done it—& they never would. ("Levi Richards, Journal, 11 June 1843, extract," p. [16], josephsmithpapers.org/paper-summary/levi-richards-journal-11-june-1843-extract/2.)

Alexander Neibaur

Alexander Neibaur (1808–1883) was born in France and was baptized in 1838. He was educated as a rabbi and was known as the first Jew to join the Church. He was fluent in seven languages and helped Joseph Smith study German and Hebrew. Neibaur first heard Joseph's testimony in 1844 during a visit to the Smith home.

24 [May 1844] called at Br J— S met Mr Bonnie— Br Joseph told us the first call he had [received] at revival meeting his Mother & Br & Sister got religion, he wanted to get religion too wanted to feel & shout like the rest but could feel nothing, opened his Bible the first passage that struck him was if any man lack wisdom let him ask of God who giveth to all men liberally & upbraideth not

went into the wood to pray knelt himself down his tongue was closed cleaved to his roof—could utter not a word, felt easier after a while—saw a fire towards heaven came near & nearer saw a personage in the fire [with a] light complexion blue eyes a piece of white cloth drawn over his shoulders his right arm bear after a while another person came to the side of the first

Mr Smith then asked must I join the Methodist Church—

No—they are not my people, all have gone astray there is none that doeth good no not one, but this is my Beloved Son harken ye him, the fire drew nigher rested upon the tree enveloped him

[illegible] comforted [him. He] endeavored to arise but felt uncommon feeble— got into the house told [his mother. He told] the Methodist priest, [who] said this was not an age for God to reveal himself in vision revelation has ceased with the New Testament. ("Alexander Neibaur, Journal, 24 May 1844, extract," p. [23], josephsmithpapers.org/paper-summary/alexander-neibaur-journal-24-may-1844-extract/1.)

Orson Pratt

Orson Pratt (1811–1881) first met Joseph Smith in 1830 and was called to be an apostle in 1835. Elder Pratt lived in the Smith home for a time and said that he had "often heard" Joseph tell the story of the First Vision. Orson Pratt taught the First Vision more frequently than any of his contemporaries. (See Journal of Discourses, *7:220–221; 11:65–66; 12:302; 14:150–141; 15:180–182.)*

Mr Joseph Smith, jun., who made the following important discovery [plates from which the Book of Mormon was translated], was born in the town of Sharon, Windsor county, Vermont, on the 23d of December, a.d. 1805. When ten years old, his parents, with their family, moved to Palmyra, New York; in the vicinity of which he resided for about eleven years, the latter part in the town of Manchester. Cultivating the earth for a livelihood was his occupation, in which he employed the most of his time. His advantages, for acquiring literary knowledge, were exceedingly small; hence, his education was limited to a slight acquaintance with two or three of the common branches of learning. He could read without much difficulty, and write a very imperfect hand; and had a very limited understanding of the ground rules of arithmetic. These were his highest and only attainments; while the rest of those branches, so universally taught in the common schools throughout the United States, were entirely unknown to him.

When somewhere about fourteen or fifteen years old, he began seriously to reflect upon the necessity of being prepared for a future state of existence: but how, or in what way, to prepare himself, was a question, as yet, undetermined in his own mind: he perceived that it was a question of infinite importance, and that the salvation of his soul depended upon a correct understanding of the same. He saw, that if he understood not the way, it would be impossible to walk in it, except by chance; and the thought of resting his hopes of eternal life upon chance, or uncertainties, was more than he could endure. If he went to the religious denominations to seek information, each one pointed to its particular tenets, saying—"This is the way, walk ye in it;" while, at the same time, the doctrines of each were, in many respects, in direct opposition to one another. It, also, occurred to his mind, that God was not the author of but one doctrine, and therefore could not acknowledge but one denomination as his church; and that such denomination must be a people, who believe, and teach, that one doctrine, (whatever it may be,) and build upon the same. He then reflected upon the immense number of doctrines, now, in the world, which had given rise to many hundreds of different denominations. The great question to be decided in his mind, was—if any one of these denominations be the Church of Christ, which one is it? Until he could become satisfied, in relation to this question, he could not rest contented. To trust to the decisions of fallible man, and build his hopes upon the same, without any certainty, and knowledge, of his own, would not satisfy the anxious desires that pervaded his breast. To decide, without any positive and definite evidence, on which he could rely, upon a subject involving the future welfare of his soul, was revolting to his feelings.

The only alternative, that seemed to be left him, was to read the Scriptures, and endeavour to follow their directions. He, accordingly, commenced perusing the sacred pages of the Bible, with sincerity, believing the things that he read. His mind soon caught hold of the following passage:—"If any of you lack wisdom, let him ask of God, that giveth to all *men* liberally, and upbraideth not; and it shall be given him."—James i. 5. From this promise he learned, that it was the privilege of all men to ask God for wisdom, with the sure and certain expectation of receiving, liberally; without being upbraided for so doing. This was cheering information to him: tidings that gave him great joy. It was like a light shining forth in a dark place, to guide him to the path in which he should walk. He, now, saw that if he inquired of God, there was, not only, a possibility, but a probability; yea, more, a certainty, that he should obtain a knowledge, which, of all the doctrines, was the doctrine of Christ; and, which, of all the churches, was the church of Christ.

He, therefore, retired to a secret place, in a grove, but a short distance from his father's house, and knelt down, and began to call upon the Lord. At first, he was severely tempted by the powers of darkness, which endeavoured to overcome him; but he continued to seek for deliverance, until darkness gave way from his mind; and he was enabled to pray, in fervency of the spirit, and in faith. And, while thus pouring out his soul, anxiously desiring an answer from God, he, at length, saw a very bright and glorious light in the heavens above; which, at first, seemed to be at a considerable distance. He continued praying, while the light appeared to be gradually descending towards him; and, as it drew nearer, it increased in brightness, and magnitude, so that, by the time that it reached the tops of the trees, the whole wilderness, for some distance around, was illuminated in a most glorious and brilliant manner. He expected to have seen the leaves and boughs of the trees consumed, as soon as the light came in contact with them; but, perceiving that it did not produce that effect, he was encouraged with the hopes of being able to endure its presence. It continued descending, slowly, until it rested upon the earth, and he was enveloped in the midst of it. When it first came upon him, it produced a peculiar sensation throughout his whole system; and, immediately, his mind was caught away, from the natural objects with which he was surrounded; and he was enwrapped in a heavenly vision, and saw two glorious personages, who exactly resembled each other in their features or likeness.

He was informed, that his sins were forgiven. He was also informed upon the subjects, which had for some time previously agitated his mind, viz.—that all the religious denominations were believing in incorrect doctrines; and, consequently, that none of them was acknowledged of God, as his church and kingdom. And he was expressly commanded, to go not after them; and he received a promise that the true doctrine—the fulness of the gospel, should, at some future time, be made known to him; after which, the vision withdrew, leaving his mind in a state of calmness and peace, indescribable. (Pratt, *An Interesting Account of Several Remarkable Visions* [1840], 3–5. This is the earliest published version of the vision.)

When, where, and how were you, Joseph Smith, first called? . . . I will give you a brief history as it came from his own mouth. I have often heard him relate it.

He was wrought upon by the Spirit of God, and felt the necessity of repenting of his sins and serving God. He retired from his father's house a little way, and bowed himself down in the wilderness, and called upon the name of the Lord. . . . In this cloud of light he saw two glorious personages; and one, pointing to the other, said, "Behold My Beloved Son. Hear ye Him!" Then he was instructed and informed in regard to many things pertaining to his own welfare, and commanded not to unite himself to any of those churches. He was also informed that at some future time the fulness of the Gospel should be made manifest to him, and he should be an instrument in the hands of God of laying the foundation of the kingdom of God. (*Journal of Discourses,* 7:220–221.)

The Lord revealed Himself to [Joseph Smith], not in his manhood, but in his youth. . . . He was about fourteen years and four months old. . . .

What were the circumstances that enabled him to have manifestations from Heaven at that early period of his life? He was very anxious, as most of mankind are, to be saved; and he was also very anxious to understand how to be saved. But on this point he was at a loss, he did not understand the way to be saved. He was a farmer's boy; he was not brought up and educated in high schools, academies or colleges; he was merely a poor farmer's boy. . . . When he was about fourteen years old there was what is called a religious revival or reformation in the neighborhood in which he lived. It was not confined to any one particular sect. The Methodists, Baptists, Presbyterians, and the various denominations in that district or country were all engaged, more or less, in this revival. Several of the relatives of this youth had taken part in this revival, and had united themselves with the Presbyterian church. This young man was also requested to unite himself with this church. First one and then another of the different persuasions would come and converse with him and try to influence him to join his lot with them; and seeing so much confusion, each sect claiming that they were the true people of God, he became at a loss what to do. He occasionally devoted an hour, when his labors on the farm would permit, to reading the Bible, and while doing so his eyes happened to fall on a certain passage of scripture, recorded in the epistle of James, which says that if any man lack wisdom let him ask of God who giveth liberally to all men and upbraideth not. Now this youth . . . was just simple enough to believe that that passage really meant what it said. He went out into a little grove near his father's house, . . . and there he knelt down in all the simplicity of a child and prayed to the Father in the name of Jesus that He would show him which, among all the churches, was the true one. Said he, "show me, Father, who are in possession of the truth, let me know, O Lord, the right way, and I will walk therein."

He had now come to a Person who was able to teach him. . . . Did the Lord hear him? Yes. But he had to exercise faith. This young man, while thus praying, was not discouraged because he was tempted; but he continued praying until he overcame the powers of darkness which tried to prevent him from calling upon God. The Lord hearkened. Being the same God who lived in ancient times, He was able to hear and answer prayers that were offered up in this sincere manner, and He answered the prayers of this youth. The heavens, as it were, were opened to him, or in other words, a glorious pillar of light like the brightness of the sun appeared in the heavens above him, and approached the spot where he was praying; his eyes were fixed upon it and his heart was lifted up in prayer before the Most High. He saw the light gradually approaching him until it rested upon the tops of the trees. He beheld that the leaves of the trees were not consumed by it, although its brightness, apparently, was sufficient, as he at first thought, to consume everything before it. But the trees were not consumed by it, and it continued to descend until it rested upon him and enveloped him in its glorious rays. When he was thus encircled about with this pillar of fire his mind was caught away from every object that surrounded him, and he was filled with the visions of the Almighty, and he saw, in the midst of this glorious pillar of fire, two glorious personages, whose countenances shone with an exceeding great luster. One of them spoke to him, saying, while pointing to the other, "This is my beloved Son in whom I am well pleased, hear ye him."

Now here was a certainty; here was something that he saw and heard; here were personages capable of instructing him, and of telling him which was the true religion. How different this from going to an uninspired man professing to be a minister! One minute's instruction from personages clothed with the glory of God coming down from the eternal worlds is worth more than all the volumes that ever were written by uninspired men.

Mr. Smith, this young man, in the simplicity of his heart, continued saying to these personages, "which church shall I join, which is the true church?" He then and there was commanded, in the most strict manner, to go not after them, for they had all gone out of the way; he was told there was no Christian church on the face of the earth according to the ancient pattern, as recorded in the New Testament; but they had all strayed from the ancient faith and had lost the gifts and power of the Holy Ghost; they had lost the spirit of revelation and prophecy, the power to heal the sick, and every other gift and blessing possessed and enjoyed by the ancient Church. "Go not after them," was the command given to this young man; and he was told that if he would be faithful in serving the true and living God, it should be made manifest to him, in a time to come, the true church that God intended to establish. (*Journal of Discourses*, 12:353–355.)

[Joseph Smith] went out to pray, being then a little over fourteen years of age, in a little grove not far from his father's house. The great object which he had in praying was to learn some few principles, which he saw were absolutely necessary to know, according to his understanding, in order to serve the true and living God. He desired to know which, among all the denominations with which he was surrounded, was the true church.

It is not often that boys of this age would be so exercised, but this was the fact in regard to Joseph Smith. He was uneducated; he had not been to college; he was not trained in the vices of all large cities; but merely a country boy accustomed to hard work with his father. . . . He heard a great many different doctrines advocated by ministers respecting the different denominations, which caused him to read the Bible. He happened to fall upon a certain passage contained in the Book of James, "If any man lack wisdom, let him ask of God, who giveth liberally and upbraideth not." This passage, when he read it, seemed to sink with great weight upon his mind. He thought it was his privilege to go to the Lord and ask him respecting the desired information. . . .

He went into the grove with a determination to claim this promise. When he was thus praying he saw a light which appeared to be approaching him from the heavens. As it came nearer it seemed to grow brighter until it settled upon the tops of the trees. He thought it would consume the leaves of the trees; but it gradually descended and rested upon him. His mind was immediately caught away. He saw in this light two glorious personages, one of whom spoke to him, pointing to the other, saying, "This is my beloved Son, hear ye him." This was a glorious vision given to this boy. When these persons interrogated him to know what he desired, he answered and said, "Lord show me which is the true church." He was then informed by one of these personages that there was no true church upon the face of the whole earth; that the whole Christian world, for many generations, had been in apostasy; that they had denied communication and revelation from heaven; denied the administration of angels; denied the power that was in the ancient church that comes through the gift of the Holy Ghost, and gave him much instruction upon this point, but did not see proper upon that occasion to give him a full knowledge of the Gospel, and what was necessary to constitute a true church, and gave him some few commandments to govern him in future time, with a promise that if he would abide the same and call upon his name, that the day would come when the Lord would reveal to him still further, making manifest what was necessary to the constitution of the true church.

The vision withdrew; the personages attending and the light withdrew. He returned to his father's house, and told the vision, not only to his parents and neighbors, but to some of the preachers of the religious denominations in that place. He was expressly commanded in the vision to unite himself to none of these churches. When he related that which he had received in this vision, the ministers immediately made light of it, and said to him, "God does not reveal anything in our days; he revealed all that was necessary in ancient times; he has not spoken for 1,800 years to anyone." From that time forth he was persecuted, not only by ministers, but all denominations in that region persecuted him. "There goes that visionary boy." This seemed to be the feeling manifested, not only by professors, but by all; but yet he knew that God had manifested himself to him; he could not be persuaded to the contrary, any more than Paul could when he heard Jesus in his first vision. (*Journal of Discourses*, 14:140–141.)

The first vision that [Joseph Smith] had was in answer to prayer. Being but a youth, and anxious for the salvation of his soul, he secretly prayed, in the wilderness, that the Lord would show unto him what he should do, what church he should join. The Lord heard and answered this prayer. Do not be astonished, good Christians, because the Lord hears prayer in the nineteenth century. . . .

Joseph Smith . . . prayed, really believing in his heart that the Lord would answer him, for he wanted wisdom, he wanted to know which was the true Christian Church, that he might be united with it; and while pleading with and praying to the Lord for this information, which was a matter of great concern to him, the heavens were opened, and two personages clothed in light or fire descended and stood before him. . . .

He was informed that there was no true Christian church on the earth, that there was no people established or organized according to the Apostolic order; that all had gone out of the way and had departed from the ancient order of things; that they had denied the power of Godliness, the gifts, miracles, the spirit of revelation and prophecy, visions, that all these things had been done away with by the unbelief of the children of men, and that there were no prophets or inspired men on the earth, as there always had been when there was a true Church upon the earth. He was strictly commanded to join none of them.

The Lord also informed him that, at some future period of time, if he would be faithful in giving heed to the instructions which were then imparted to him, and in his prayers to the Lord, he would impart to him his own doctrine in plainness and simplicity. (*Journal of Discourses*, 15:181–182.)

Mr. Smith had this vision before he was fifteen years old, and, immediately after receiving it, he began to relate it to some of his nearest friends, and he was told by some of the ministers who came to him to enquire about it, that there was no such thing as the visitation of heavenly messengers, that God gave no new revelation, and that no visions could be given to the children of men in this age. This was like telling him that there was no such thing as seeing, or feeling, or hearing, or tasting, or smelling. Why? Because he knew positively to the contrary; he knew that he had seen this light, that he had beheld these two personages, and that he had heard the voice of one of them; he also knew that he had received instruction from them, and therefore, to be told that there was no such thing as revelation or vision in these days, was like telling him that the sun did not shine in these days. He knew to the contrary, and he continued to testify that God had made himself manifest to him; and in consequence of this, the prejudices of the different denominations were aroused against him.

Why should they feel such concern and anxiety in relation to his testimony as to persecute him, a boy not quite fifteen years of age? The reason was obvious—if that testimony was true, not one of their churches was the true Church of Christ. No wonder, then, that they began to persecute, point the finger of scorn, and say—"There goes the visionary boy." (*Journal of Discourses*, 17:279–280.)

God . . . had given revelation to this youth on many occasions. The first one that he gave to him was in the spring of 1820, before Joseph Smith was of the age of fifteen. Then a wonderful revelation was given to him, the first one he ever received. In a great and glorious open vision, in answer to his prayers, there was the manifestation of two of the great personages in the heavens—not angels, not messengers, but two persons that hold the keys of authority over all the creations of the universe.

Who were they? God the Eternal Father and his Son Jesus Christ, through whom God the Father made the worlds! These glorious personages descended from heaven; two personages whose countenances outshone the sun at noonday; two personages clothed with a pillar of light round about them, descended, stood before this lad, and revealed themselves to him. He saw their countenances; he saw the glory of their personages; he heard the glorious words that proceeded from the Father, as he pointed to his Son and said, to Joseph, "This is My Beloved Son in whom I am well pleased." This was a new revelation; something different from what had been made manifest for a great many centuries, according to the declarations of the articles and creeds of men. (*Journal of Discourses*, 21:308–309.)

"No man without the Priesthood, can behold the face of the Father and live."

Now, this has troubled the minds of some of the Latter-day Saints. "How is it, (say they) that Joseph lived, after having seen the face of the Father, after having heard the words of His mouth, after the Father had said unto him, 'He is my beloved Son, hear ye him.'"

If you had thought upon this other subject, namely, that Joseph had been already ordained before this world was made — to what Priesthood? To the Priesthood after the Order of . . . His Only Begotten Son. If you had only reflected that that same Priesthood had been conferred upon him in the councils of the holy ones before the world was made, and that he was ordained to come forth in this dispensation of the fulness of times to hold the keys of authority and power of that high and holy Priesthood — that he was ordained to come forth and perform the work that God intended to accomplish in the latter times, then the mystery would have been cleared up to your minds. He was not without the Priesthood in reality; but was a man chosen, a man ordained, a man appointed from before the foundation of this world, to come forth in the fulness of times to introduce the last dispensation among the children of men; to come in order to organize that kingdom, that was predicted by the ancient Prophets, that should stand forever; to come to fulfil the great and glorious work of preparation for the coming of the Son of God to reign in righteousness upon the earth; he could see the face of God the Father and live. (*Journal of Discourses*, 22:29–30.)

Orson Hyde

Orson Hyde (1805–1878) joined the Church in 1831 and then served a mission with Hyrum and Samuel Smith. He was called to be an apostle in 1835. He served as president of the Quorum of the Twelve for nearly thirty years.

Joseph Smith jun[ior], the person to whom the angel of the Lord was first sent, was born on December 23 in the year of our Lord 1805 in the town of Sharon, Windsor County, Vermont. When he was ten years old, his parents moved to Palmyra in the state of New York. For almost eleven years he lived here [in Palmyra] and in the neighboring town of Manchester. His only occupation was to plow and cultivate the soil. Because his parents were poor and had to feed a large family, his education was meager. He was able to read fairly well, but his ability to write was very limited and had only little literary knowledge. His knowledge of letters did not go any further. Most of the subjects which were generally taught in the United States of America were completely unknown to him at the time he was favored with a heavenly message.

When he had reached his fifteenth year, he began to think seriously about the importance of preparing for a future [existence]; but it was very difficult for him to decide how he should go about such an important undertaking. He recognized clearly that it would be impossible for him to walk the proper path without being acquainted with it beforehand; and to base his hopes for eternal life on chance or blind uncertainty would have been more than he had ever been inclined to do. . . .

Consequently he began in an attitude of faith his own investigation of the word of God [feeling that it was] the best way to arrive at a knowledge of the truth. He had not proceeded very far in this laudable endeavor when his eyes fell upon the following verse of St. James [1:5]: "If any of you lack wisdom, let him ask of God, that giveth to all men liberally, and upbraideth not; and it shall be given him." He considered this scripture an authorization for him to solemnly call upon his creator to present his needs before him with the certain expectation of some success. And so he began to pour out to the Lord with fervent determination the earnest desires of his soul.

On one occasion, he went to a small grove of trees near his father's home and knelt down before God in solemn prayer. The adversary then made several strenuous efforts to cool his ardent soul. He filled his mind with doubts and brought to mind all manner of inappropriate images to prevent him from obtaining the object of his endeavors; but the overflowing mercy of God came to buoy him up and gave new impetus to his failing strength. However, the dark cloud soon parted and light and peace filled his frightened heart. Once again he called upon the Lord with faith and fervency of spirit.

At this sacred moment, the natural world around him was excluded from his view, so that he would be open to the presentation of heavenly and spiritual things. Two glorious heavenly personages stood before him, resembling each other exactly in features and stature. They told him that his prayers had been answered and that the Lord had decided to grant him a special blessing. He was also told that he should not join any of the religious sects or denominations, because all of them erred in doctrine and none was recognized by God as his church and kingdom. He was further commanded, to wait patiently until some future time, when the true doctrine of Christ and the complete truth of the gospel would be revealed to him. The vision closed and peace and calm filled his mind. (Orson Hyde, *A Cry out of the Wilderness* [1842], 13–30; English translation by Marvin H. Folsom.)

John Taylor

John Taylor (1808–1887) was born in England, joined the Church in 1836, and was called to be an apostle in 1838. He was present with Joseph Smith at the martyrdom, being severely wounded during the attack. President Taylor became the leader of the church in 1877.

[Joseph Smith's] mind was troubled, he saw contention instead of peace; and division instead of union; and when he reflected upon the multifarious creeds and professions there were in existence, he thought it impossible for all to be right, and if God taught one, He did not teach the others, "for God is not the author of confusion." In reading his bible, he was remarkably struck with the passage in James, 1st chapter, 5th verse, "If any of you lack wisdom, let him ask of God, that giveth to all men liberally and upbraideth not, and it shall be given him." Believing in the word of God, he retired into a grove, and called upon the Lord to give him wisdom in relation to this matter. While he was thus engaged, he was surrounded by a brilliant light, and two glorious personages presented themselves before him, who exactly resembled each other in features, and who gave him information upon the subjects which had previously agitated his mind. He was given to understand that the churches were all of them in error in regard to many things; and he was commanded not to go after them; and he received a promise that the "fulness" of the gospel should at some future time be unfolded unto him: after which the vision withdrew, leaving his mind in a state of calmness and peace. (*Millennial Star*, 1850, 235–236.)

Who among the nations of the earth knew or comprehended anything about the government of God? None did; nowhere; no king, no emperor, no potentate, no president, no power upon the face of the earth; no divine or theologian, no scientist, no philosopher, understood anything about this matter. It is indeed the kingdom of God, and being his kingdom, it must originate with him, it must receive from him its teachings, its forms, its principles, its laws, its ordinances, its institutions, and everything connected therewith must emanate from God. . . . You cannot teach a child algebra, nor arithmetic, until it has gone through a certain system of training. You cannot teach the arts and sciences without necessary preparation for their introduction, nor can you teach people in the government of God without they are placed in communication with him. . . .

Hence as a commencement the Lord appeared unto Joseph Smith, both the Father and the Son, the Father pointing to the Son said, "This is My Beloved Son in whom I am well pleased, Hear ye Him!" Here, then, was a communication from the heavens made known unto man on the earth, and he at that time came into possession of a fact that no man knew in the world but he, and that is that God lived, for he had seen him, and that his Son Jesus Christ lived, for he also had seen him. What next? Now says the Father, "This is my beloved Son, hear him." . . . He, the Son of God, the Savior of the world, the Redeemer of man, he was the one pointed out to be the guide, the director, the instructor, and the leader in the development of the great principles of that kingdom and that government which he then commenced to institute. (*Journal of Discourses*, 21:64–65.)

George A. Smith

George A. Smith (1817–1875) was a first cousin to Joseph Smith. He was called to be an apostle in 1839 and later served in the First Presidency under Brigham Young.

Joseph Smith, jun., was born in Sharon, Windsor county, Vermont, 23d December, 1805; moved with his father to Ontario county, New York, and in the year 1819 resided in Manchester; he was by occupation a farmer, and his advantages of education were limited.

At the age of 15 he began to reflect seriously on the necessity of being prepared for a future state of existence. He went among the different denominations that existed in that state, and his mind became perplexed with the clashing and contention which existed among those who professed the name of Christ.

Disgusted with the confusion which his researches disclosed, and encouraged by the promise of Saint James: "If any of you lack wisdom, let him ask of God who giveth unto all men liberally and upbraideth not, and it shall be given him," he retired to a grove, and in earnest prayer besought the Lord to reveal the way of salvation; and while thus engaged he beheld two glorious Beings wrapped in a brilliant and glorious light, who informed him that all the religious sects of the present age had departed from the ancient gospel of Jesus Christ and his apostles, with its gifts and priesthood, which should be made known to him in due season: many glorious things were shown him in this vision. (*Deseret News*, 5 Sept. 1855, 2.)

Brigham Young

Brigham Young (1801–1877) joined the Church in 1832 and was called to be an apostle in 1835. One of Joseph Smith's closest associates, Brigham led the church from 1844 to his death in 1877.

When the Lord called upon Joseph he was but a boy—a child, only about fourteen years of age. He was not filled with traditions; his mind was not made up to this, that, or the other. I very well recollect the reformation which took place in the country among the various denominations of Christians—the Baptists, Methodists, Presbyterians, and others—when Joseph was a boy. . . . Joseph was naturally inclined to be religious, and being young, and surrounded with this excitement, no wonder that he became seriously impressed with the necessity of serving the Lord. But as the cry on every hand was, "Lo, here is Christ," and "Lo, there!" Said he, "Lord, teach me, that I may know for myself, who among these are right."

And what was the answer? "They are all out of the way; they have gone astray, and there is none that doeth good, no not one."

When he found out that none were right, he began to inquire of the Lord what was right, and he learned for himself. Was he aware of what was going to be done? By no means. He did not know what the Lord was going to do with him, although He had informed him that the Christian churches were all wrong, because they had not the Holy Priesthood, and had strayed from the holy commandments of the Lord, precisely as the children of Israel did. (*Journal of Discourses*, 12:70.)

I never saw any one, until I met Joseph Smith, who could tell me anything about the character personality and dwelling-place of God, or anything satisfactory about angels, or the relationship of man to his Maker. . . .

I know that Joseph Smith was a Prophet of God, and that he had many revelations. Who can disprove this testimony? Any one may dispute it, but there is no one in the world who can disprove it. (*Journal of Discourses*, 16:46.)

George Q. Cannon

George Q. Cannon (1827–1901) joined the Church in 1840 and was called to be an apostle in 1860. He served in the First Presidency under four successive presidents of the church, from Brigham Young to Lorenzo Snow. Cannon was a nephew of John Taylor.

Joseph Smith, inspired of God, came forth and declared that God lived. Ages had passed and no one had beheld Him. The fact that he existed was like a dim tradition in the minds of the people. The fact that Jesus lived was only supposed to be the case because eighteen hundred years before men had seen him. . . . The character of God—whether He was a personal being, whether His center was nowhere, and His circumference everywhere, were matters of speculation. No one had seen him. No one had seen any one who had seen an angel. . . . Is it a wonder that men were confused? that there was such a variety of opinion respecting the character and being of God? . . .

Brother Joseph, as I said, startled the world. It stood aghast at the statement which he made, and the testimony which he bore. He declared that he had seen God. He declared that he had seen Jesus Christ.

After that revelation faith began to grow up in men's minds and hearts. Speculation concerning the being of God ceased among those who received the testimony of Joseph Smith. He testified that God was a being of body, that He had a body, that man was in his likeness, that Jesus was the exact counterpart of the Father, and that the Father and Jesus were two distinct personages, as distinct as an earthly father and an earthly son. (*Journal of Discourses,* 24:340–341.)

When the set time had come for God to reestablish His Church and to bring to pass the fulfillment of that which had been spoken by the mouths of the Prophets, He came himself.

The first account we have of the visitation of divine beings in this dispensation is the account that is given to us by the Prophet Joseph Smith himself, concerning the visit of the Father and the Son. There had been men, doubtless many men in the various ages of the world, who had light and who had a degree of the Spirit of God. . . . I believe many men were inspired who . . . did not have the Holy Priesthood, but were led by the Spirit of God to strive for a better condition of affairs and to live a purer and higher life than those by whom they were surrounded were living. But while this was the case it was the Spirit of God that did it.

We have no account—no authenticated account at least—of angels coming from heaven, or of the Father manifesting Himself unto the children of men. . . . The first that we knew concerning God was through the testimony of the Prophet Joseph.

Even the personality of God was doubted. The traditions of men were so false respecting God that the idea of a personal Deity had faded from the so-called Christian mind. . . . There was no man scarcely upon the earth that had a true conception of God; the densest ignorance prevailed; and even ministers of religion could not conceive of the true idea, and there was mystery associated with what is called the Trinity—that is, with the Father, the Son, and the Holy Ghost.

But all this was swept away in one moment by the appearance of the Almighty Himself—by the appearance of God, the Father, and His Son Jesus Christ, to the boy Joseph . . . one moment all this darkness disappeared, and once more there was a man found on the earth, embodied in the flesh, who had seen God, who had seen Jesus, and who could describe the personality of both. Faith was again restored to the earth, the true faith and the true knowledge concerning our Creator . . . This revelation dissipated all misconceptions and all false ideas, and removed the uncertainty that had existed respecting these matters. The Father came accompanied by the Son, thus showing that there were two personages of the Godhead, two presiding personages whom we worship and to whom we look, the one the Father and the other the Son. Joseph saw that the Father a form; that He had a head; that He had arms; that He had limbs; that He had feet; that He had a face and a tongue with which to express His thoughts; for He said unto Joseph: "This is my beloved Son"—pointing to the Son—"hear Him."

Now, it was meant that this knowledge should be restored first of all. It seems so, at least, from the fact that God Himself came; it seems that the knowledge had to be restored the basis for all true faith to be built upon. There can be no faith that is not built upon true conception of God our Father. Therefore, before even angels came, He came himself, accompanied by His Son, and revealed Himself once more to man upon the earth.

As I have said, the set time had come, the instrument had been born—the instrument that had been selected doubtless as much as the Son of God had been selected to accomplish His mission— that is, He had also been selected from before the foundation of the world, to come and to be the instrument in the hands of God to again lay the foundation of His Church upon the earth—that instrument had been born and the set time had come for the establishment of the work of the Lord. Joseph Smith had the necessary gifts and qualifications by which he was enabled to seek unto God with such irresistible faith that God heard his prayer and granted unto him the desire of his heart by revealing Himself unto him and giving unto him the instructions which He did. (*Journal of Discourses*, 24:371–372.)

The first quarter of the nineteenth century was a time of intense religious excitement, and New York and surrounding states were the scenes of many revivals and much strife. Not only among preachers and exhorters was the enthusiasm manifested, but the people themselves became much exercised over their sinful condition, and ran here and there in a wild search for the salvation for which their souls seemed to yearn. The movement originated with the Methodists; but it soon spread to other sects in the neighborhood, until the whole region was infected by it, and the greatest excitement was created, in which all the good effects of a revival were swallowed up in bitter contests of opinions and the strife of words between the adherents of the various creeds.

The Smith family inclined towards the Presbyterian faith, and the mother, two sons and a daughter united themselves with that church. Joseph was at the time in his fifteenth year—just at an age, with his limited experience, he might be deemed most susceptible to the example of others. He listened and considered, yet could not profess the faith of his family. The clergymen of other sects assailed him; but although he became somewhat partial to the Methodist creed, their soft words and direful threats were alike unavailing. The tempest could not reach the depths of the boy's nature. Unknown to himself he was awaiting the hour when the divine message should stir the waters of his soul.

. . . The all-absorbing question with him was: Which of these churches is the church of Christ? . . .

Searching the scriptures for comfort and light, one happy and most fortunate moment he read these sacred words:

"If any of you lack wisdom, let him ask of God, that giveth to all men liberally, and upbraideth not; and it shall be given him."

Like a flash of sunlight through lowering clouds, the import of a mighty truth burst upon Joseph's mind. He had been vainly asking help from men who had answered him out of their own darkness. He determined now to seek assistance from God. . . .

There was the plain promise. He could not doubt it, without doubting his Maker. He felt that he lacked wisdom; and to such as he, asking of God, there was the divine pledge to hear and give without upbraiding.

It was one morning in early springtime of the year 1820, that Joseph felt the earnest prompting and adopted the holy resolve. He walked into the depths of a wood, which stood near his home, and sought a little glade. There, in trembling humility, but with a faith which thrilled his soul—alone, unseen of man, he fell upon his knees and lifted his voice in prayer to God.

While he was calling upon the Almighty, a subtle and malignant power seized him and stilled his utterance. Deep darkness enveloped him; he felt that he was in the grasp of Satan, and that the destroyer was exerting all the power of hell to drag him to sudden destruction.

In his agony he called anew upon the Lord for deliverance; and at the moment when he seemed to be sinking under the power of the evil one, the deep gloom was rolled away and he saw a brilliant light. A pillar of celestial fire, far more glorious than the brightness of the noon-day sun, appeared directly above him. The defeated power fled with the darkness; and Joseph's spirit was free to worship and marvel at his deliverance. Gradually the light descended until it rested upon him; and he saw, standing above him in the air, enveloped in the pure radiance of the fiery pillar, two personages of incomparable beauty, alike in form and feature, and clad alike in snowy raiment. Sublime, dazzling, they filled his soul with awe. At length, One, calling Joseph by name, stretched His shining arm towards the other, and said:

"This is my Beloved Son: Hear Him!"

As soon as Joseph could regain possession of himself, to which he was encouraged by the benign and comforting look of the Son, and by the heavenly bliss which pervaded his own soul, he found words to ask, which of all the multitude of churches upon the face of the globe had the gospel of Christ; for up to this time it had never entered his mind to doubt that the true church of the Lamb, pure and undefiled, had an existence somewhere among men.

But the answer came that no one of the creeds of earth was pure, and that Joseph must unite himself with none of them. Said the glorious Being:

"They draw near me with their lips, but their hearts are far from me; they teach for the doctrine the commandments of men, having a form of godliness, but they deny the power thereof."

. . . The Heavenly Personages continued to commune with him, and repeated Their command that he should not ally himself with any of the man-made sects. Then They and Their enclosing pillar of light passed from his gaze, and he was left to look into the immensity of space.

The boy's faith in the promises of God had now deepened into knowledge. He had been assailed by the power of evil, until it seemed he must succumb—that the limit of human endurance was passed. And in that instant of deepest despair, he had been suddenly transported into the blaze of celestial light. He had seen with his own eyes the Father and the Son, with his own ears he had heard Their eternal voice. Over this untaught youth at least, the Heavens were no longer as brass. He had emerged from the maze of doubt and uncertainty in which he had so long groped, and had received positive assurances on the matter nearest his heart from Him, whom to know was anciently declared to be life eternal.

Emboldened, satisfied, and happy beyond expression, Joseph's first thought was of his loved ones. He must impart the glorious truth to them. His parents and his brethren listened, and were lost in awe at his straightforward recital. He next sought his old friends the ministers, those who had affected such an interest in his welfare and who would nave so willingly acted as his guides toward heaven. His first experience with these gentlemen was somewhat discouraging. A Methodist preacher who had formerly cultivated the utmost friendship, and who probably had acquired considerable influence with him, was soon informed by Joseph of the Heavenly manifestation. The pious man treated the communication with contempt, and curtly replied that there were no such things as visions or revelations in these days, they having ceased with the Apostles, and that the whole thing was of the Devil. Other ministers, and in fact the religious portion of the entire neighborhood, as the event became more widely known, united in the determination to overwhelm with ridicule and abuse that which they found themselves unable to silence by argument.

Joseph had been a great favorite among his neighbors, his gentle ways had made him beloved by all; he now was hated and reviled. He had been especially sought after by the clergy because of his diligence, earnestness and humility in striving to secure the grace of God; he now was stigmatized as a dissolute dreamer, a worthless knave and an arrant hypocrite. A boy of fourteen is seldom the object of universal conversation and comment in his locality; yet this youth's enemies did not rest short of lifting him to an eminence where he could the better be seen and scorned of all men.

His family were made to share the vindictiveness and contumely exhibited toward him which at last reached such a pitch that an attempt was actually made to assassinate him. The family, on hearing the report of the gun, rushed from the house only to find the marks made by the crouching murderer at the side of the path, and the leaden missiles embedded a short distance from the spot. But persecution, slander and cruel outrage were all unable to change the steadfast testimony of Joseph. (Cannon, *The Life of Joseph Smith the Prophet*, 2d ed. [1907], 29–33.)

It is a wonderful story to tell—wonderful in its condescension, wonderful in the glorious effects that have followed it, wonderful for this generation to hear, wonderful for us to live in an age such as this and to be so favored as we have been—that God, the Eternal Father, the Creator of heaven and earth, the Fountain of all existence and of all power, has condescended in our day to come down from heaven, from His glorious abode, accompanied by His Son, Jesus, to restore to the earth this love and these gifts, to give to men this wonderful power and these extraordinary gifts! . . .

Think of living at a time when this event so far reaching in importance to heaven and earth has taken place—the Father Himself, accompanied by His Son Jesus Christ, condescending to come from heaven to usher in this dispensation and to prepare the way for the restoration of that authority by which He Himself acts and governs all things! (Stuy, *Collected Discourses* [1999], 5:22.)

Wilford Woodruff

Wilford Woodruff (1807–1898) joined the Church in 1833 and was called to be an apostle in 1838. He served as fourth president of the Church beginning in 1889.

A greater prophet than he [Joseph Smith], excepting Jesus Christ, I do not believe ever lived. In saying this I give it as my own personal views. I don't believe God ever raised up a greater prophet, save Jesus himself. . . . Our testimony of him is that he was taught of God Himself and of the angels who visited him. (Stuy, *Collected Discourses* [1999], 1:383.)

The Lord raised up Joseph Smith. He came forth in the proper time. He organized a Church. Who was Joseph Smith? Was he a lawyer? Was he a doctor of divinity? Was he what is called a great man, a learned man? No, he was but a youth; the world would say an illiterate, ignorant youth. He was an unlearned youth in the things of the world. But he was a pure man. He came forth through the lineage of Abraham, Isaac and Jacob. He was prophesied of by the ancient Patriarchs and Prophets. The Book of Mormon gives his name.

Joseph Smith was moved upon by the Holy Ghost, and he was administered unto, in answer to his prayers, by the Father and the Son; and the Father said to him, "This is my beloved Son, hear ye Him." He listened strictly to the words of Jesus Christ, and continued to do so until he, like the Savior, was put to death. (Stuy, *Collected Discourses* [1999], 2:285.)

Part 3

TESTIMONIES AND TEACHINGS

OF LATER PROPHETS AND APOSTLES

By the early years of the twentieth century, few Church members were still alive who had personally known Joseph Smith. But the power of his witness of the First Vision, given two generations earlier, continued to resonate in the personal testimonies of those who followed him. Church leaders of this later period had grown up hearing the stories of Joseph told by his closest associates, and these accounts were bolstered by the whisperings of the Holy Ghost to the hearts of those who listened.

This is fully consistent with what Joseph Smith and his associates taught in the *Lectures on Faith*. A vital element of building faith is hearing testimony from those who have had personal experience with God. Lecture 2 teaches that the only way mankind could know of "the existence of God . . . was by a manifestation of God to man."

Thus, Adam was the first who was "made acquainted with God," and then he "communicated the knowledge which he had unto his posterity; and it was through this means that the thought was first suggested to their minds that there was a God." This gave them a foundation through which they could exercise their faith, "through which they could obtain a knowledge of his character and also of his glory."

"For instance, Abel, before he received the assurance from heaven that his offerings were acceptable unto God, had received the important information of his father, that such a being did exist, who had created, and who did uphold all things." In like manner, Adam and Eve were the source of this great knowledge for all their posterity.

The lecture goes on to teach that Adam taught several generations of his posterity about God, and those men and women, in turn, taught those who followed

It's not enough, of course, to simply receive the testimony of the fathers and mothers. They can teach that God exists. But for their posterity, "the extent of their knowledge, respecting his character and glory, will depend upon their diligence and faithfulness in seeking after him, until like Enoch, the brother of Jared, and Moses, they shall obtain faith in God, and power with him to behold him face to face." (*Lectures on Faith*, 2:30–36, 43–44, 55.)

The great truth taught by Joseph Smith and others in the *Lectures on Faith* holds for this dispensation. This is seen by the way in which the memory and testimony of the First Vision passed down from generation to generation, as seen by the experiences of those who are represented in this section.

Brigham Young and the other early apostles taught those who came after:

Joseph F. Smith and Heber J. Grant both served as apostles under the first generation of Latter-day Saint leaders and both were sons of parents who helped establish the foundation of the Church. Anthon H. Lund and Rudger Clawson likewise were called by stalwart leaders who were part of the first generation of Saints: John Taylor and Lorenzo Snow. Thus, these early leaders learned at the feet of those who had directly learned from Joseph Smith.

The second generation of leaders received teachings from such powerful prophets as Wilford Woodruff, who taught, "No greater prophet than Joseph Smith ever lived on the face of the earth save Jesus Christ." (*Discourses of Wilford Woodruff* [1946], 43.)

In turn, George Albert Smith, Charles W. Penrose, David O. McKay, Orson F. Whitney, Joseph Fielding Smith, and James E.

Talmage were all called into the apostleship by Joseph F. Smith. And Melvin J. Ballard, John A. Widtsoe, Joseph F. Merrill, and J. Reuben Clark Jr. were all called to be apostles by Heber J. Grant.

Joseph F. Smith conveyed to his fellow leaders—and to the Church—a powerful testimony of his uncle, Joseph Smith. For example, he said, "[Joseph Smith] never taught a doctrine that was not true. He never practiced a doctrine that he was not commanded to practice. He never advocated error. He was not deceived. He saw; he heard; he did as he was commanded to do; and, therefore, God is responsible for the work accomplished by Joseph Smith—not Joseph Smith. The Lord is responsible for it, and not man." (*Gospel Doctrine* [1919], 627.)

As the generations passed, the tradition of testimony continued. Prophets and apostles down through the years have been taught by their predecessors—and then each received their own powerful witness of the literal reality of the First Vision of Joseph Smith. Besides those mentioned above, testimonies and teachings of the following Church presidents are included in this section: Harold B. Lee, Spencer W. Kimball, Ezra Taft Benson, Howard W. Hunter, Gordon B. Hinckley, Thomas S. Monson, and Russell M. Nelson.

And the following apostles (in addition to those mentioned above) are also included: Marion G. Romney, Hugh B. Brown, N. Eldon Tanner, Bruce R. McConkie, James E. Faust, David B. Haight, Neal A. Maxwell, M. Russell Ballard, Jeffrey R. Holland, Henry B. Eyring, and Dieter F. Uchtdorf.

The teachings and testimonies in this section are arranged with prophets listed, followed by the apostles. The prophets are included in the order of their service, with their statements in chronological order. The apostles are also listed in the order of their call, and if they have multiple statements, they are in chronological order.

Prophets
(arranged in order of their service)

Joseph F. Smith

Joseph F. Smith (1838–1918), son of Hyrum and nephew of Joseph, was only five years old at the time of the martyrdom. He was called to be an apostle in 1866 and was a counselor in First Presidency under four successive presidents of the Church. He was Church president beginning in 1901.

Joseph Smith . . . confess[ed] the great fact that he had heard the voice of God and the voice of His Son Jesus Christ, speaking to him in his childhood; that he saw those Heavenly Beings standing above him in the air of the woods where he went to pray. . . . He suffered persecution all the days of his life on earth because he declared it was true. (*Two Sermons by President Joseph F. Smith*, Sermon Tract, no. 1 [1906].)

From the day that the Prophet Joseph Smith first declared his vision until now, the enemy of all righteousness, the enemy of truth, of virtue, of honor, uprightness and purity of life, the enemy of the only true God, the enemy to direct revelation from God and to the inspirations that come from the heavens to man, has been arrayed against this work. (*Gospel Doctrine* [1919], 464.)

The greatest event that has ever occurred in the world, since the resurrection of the Son of God from the tomb and his ascension on high, was the coming of the Father and of the Son to that boy Joseph Smith, to prepare the way for the laying of the foundation of [God's] kingdom—not the kingdom of man—never more to cease nor to be overturned.

Having accepted this truth, I find it easy to accept of every

other truth that he enunciated and declared during his mission
. . . in the world. (*Gospel Doctrine* [1919], 627.)

Heber J. Grant

*Heber J. Grant (1856–1945), was the son of Jedediah M. Grant, a
counselor to Brigham Young, who passed away when Heber was two
years old. Heber was called to be an apostle at age twenty-five in 1882.
He became Church president beginning in 1918.*

We celebrate the hundredth anniversary of a marvelous occurrence fraught with wondrous results, not only to those who
lived in the day in which it took place, but to men and women of
today; and its influence will continue to be felt for good in all the
years that are to come.

The appearance of God the Father and his Son Jesus Christ to
the boy prophet Joseph Smith is the greatest event that has taken
place in all the world since the birth of our Lord and Redeemer,
Jesus Christ. It was the most wonderful vision ever bestowed
upon mortal man; for, while Jesus the Son had walked and talked
with men both before and after his resurrection, I know of no record in which we are informed that both ever appeared together
in a visit to the earth, as in this marvelous vision to Joseph Smith.

The event marks the beginning of "a marvelous work and a
wonder," which was foretold by Isaiah the Prophet (29:13, 14)
confirmed by Daniel (2:29–44), and further predicted by John the
Revelator (14:6, 7). The personal visitation of the Father and the
Son, choosing Joseph to be the leader of the Dispensation of the
Fulness of Times, marked the beginning of this work, and this
was supplemented by the visitation of angels and other holy messengers, conferring upon Joseph the powers of the Priesthood,
the authority to act in the name of God—to introduce the gospel
of Jesus Christ by divine authority to mankind, and by divine
direction to organize and establish the true Church of Christ in
the latter days. (*Improvement Era*, Apr. 1920, 472–474.)

That wonderful and marvelous vision [was] the greatest event in all the history of the world, excepting only the birth and death of the Savior. (Conference Report, Apr. 1920, 13.)

Either Joseph Smith did see God and did converse with Him, and God Himself did introduce Jesus Christ to the boy Joseph Smith, and Jesus Christ did tell Joseph Smith that he would be the instrument in the hands of God of establishing again upon the earth the true Gospel of Jesus Christ—or Mormonism, so-called, is a myth.

And Mormonism is not a myth! It is the power of God unto salvation; it is the Church of Jesus Christ, established under His direction, and all the disbelief of the world cannot change the fundamental facts connected with the Church of Jesus Christ of Latter-day Saints. (*Gospel Standards* [1943], 3.)

The most glorious thing that has ever happened in the history of the world since the Savior Himself lived on earth, is that God Himself saw fit to visit the earth with His beloved, only begotten Son, our Redeemer and Savior, and to appear to the boy Joseph. . . . There are thousands and hundreds of thousands who have had a perfect and individual testimony and knowledge of this eternal truth. (*Improvement Era,* July 1939, 393.)

George Albert Smith

George Albert Smith (1870–1951) was a son and grandson of two apostles (John H. Smith and George A. Smith). He was called to be an apostle in 1903 and president of the Church in 1945.

When the boy prophet, in the woods of Palmyra, saw the Father and the Son, and realized that they were indeed person-ages, that they could hear and reply to what he said, it began a new era in this world, and laid a foundation for the faith of the children of men. They could now pray to our Father in heaven and realize that he could hear and answer their prayers, that there was a connection between the heavens and the earth. (Conference Report, Oct. 1916, 37.)

David O. McKay

David O. McKay (1873–1970) was called to be an apostle in 1906. He served in the First Presidency under three presidents and was sustained as church president in 1951.

One hundred years ago Joseph Smith, a mere boy between fourteen and fifteen years of age, declared that in answer to prayer, he received a revelation from God. His declaration was simple, but positive; and he was surprised when men doubted the truth of his assertion. To him his claim was but the statement of a fact; to the Christian world, it was a lightning flash that shattered their religious structure, from turret to foundation.

Two important elements in his first message were these: (1) That God is a personal being, and will communicate his will to men; and (2), that no creed in Christendom had the true plan of salvation. Indeed, all were an "abomination in the sight of God, ... having a form of godliness, but denying the power thereof."

For boldness of assertion; for rejection of prevailing orthodoxy; as a challenge to professed ministers; this claim of a fair-haired, blue-eyed youth stands without parallel since the days of Jesus of Nazareth. Not even Luther's defiance, at Worms, is excepted; for his inspired effort, at first, was only to purify the church of corrupt practices; while Joseph Smith rejected the creeds as unauthoritative, and many of their doctrines as absolutely false.

And thus, by his simple declaration, he found himself alone in the religious world.

Alone—and unacquainted with the learning and philosophy of his day.

Alone—and unschooled in the arts and sciences.

Alone—with no philosopher to instruct him, no minister to

guide him. In simplicity and kindness he had hastened to them with his glorious message; in scorn and derision they had turned from him saying that it was all of the devil; that there were no such things as revelations or visions in these days; that all such things had ceased with the apostles, and that there would never be any more of them.

Alone—compelled to embark upon the ocean of religious thought, having rejected every known vessel with which to sail, and never having built one or even having seen one built himself. Surely, if an impostor, the bark he builds will be a crude one indeed.

If, on the other hand, that which he builds possesses an excellence and superiority over that which the learned men and philosophers had given to mankind during the preceding hundreds of years, the world will at least stand aside, and say in surprise, Whence hath this man his wisdom? It would seem that, though he was alone, he was alone only as was Moses on Sinai; as Jesus, on the Mt. of Olives and on other sacred places where he communed with his Father. As with the Master, so with the prophet; his instruction came not through man-made channels, but direct from God, the source of all intelligence. He said himself:

"I am a rough stone. The sound of the hammer and chisel were never heard on me until the Lord took me in hand. I desire the learning and wisdom of Heaven alone."

When Joseph Smith taught a doctrine, he taught it authoritatively. His was not a question whether his thoughts agreed with men's thoughts or not; whether they were in harmony with the teachings of the orthodox churches or whether they were in direct opposition. What was given to him he gave to the world, irrespective of its agreement or disagreement, of its harmony or its discord with the belief of the churches, or the prevailing standards of mankind. . . . The guiding spirit of his life was manifest from the beginning of his ministry and confirms his wonderful declaration that God had spoken to him. . . .

As we look through the vista of one hundred years and see the boy prophet standing alone in the midst of a tempestuously religious world, declaring that God had spoken to him, and that there was not an authorized Church of Christ upon the earth; when we know that to make good his claim, he must give to the world something superior to that produced by the philosophy of the ages and the best wisdom of man; when we realize how impotent he was to do this, if dependent upon his own learning and wisdom,—we cannot help but conclude, since he has given to the world something which has stood the acid test of time and criticism, and which stands today in brilliancy and sublimity, superior to anything proclaimed by human wisdom, that surely he was indeed the Chosen Prophet of the Latter Day. (*Improvement Era*, Apr. 1920, 506–507, 513.)

One outstandingly distinguishing feature of this Church is divine authority by direct revelation. The appearing of the Father and the Son to Joseph Smith is the foundation of this Church. Therein lies the secret of its strength and vitality. This is true, and I bear witness to it. That one revelation answers all the queries of science regarding God and his divine personality. Don't you see what that means? What God is, is answered. His relation to his children is clear. His interest in humanity through authority delegated to man is apparent. The future of the work is assured. These and other glorious truths are clarified by that glorious first vision. (*Church News*, 9 July 1952, 2.)

Joseph Fielding Smith

Joseph Fielding Smith (1887–1972) was a son of Joseph F. Smith and grandson of Hyrum Smith. He was a prolific writer of Church history and doctrine and served as assistant Church historian and Church historian from 1906 to 1970. He was called to be an apostle in 1910 and was sustained as Church president in 1970.

When Joseph Smith went in the woods to pray, just one hundred years ago, he received a revelation of knowledge, truth and power, which has been of inestimable value and blessing to the world. What was revealed to him there was given for the over-throw of false creeds and traditions of the ages and led ulti-mately to the restoration of the everlasting gospel as revealed by our Redeemer during his ministry.

For hundreds of years the world was wrapped in a veil of spir-itual darkness, until there was not one fundamental truth belong-ing to the plan of salvation that was not, in the year 1820, so ob-scured by false tradition and ceremonies, borrowed from paganism, as to make it unrecognizable; or else it was entirely denied. By heavenly direction and command of our Lord Jesus Christ, Joseph Smith restored all these principles in their primi-tive beauty and power. . . .

The vision of Joseph Smith made it clear that the Father and the Son are separate personages, having bodies as tangible as the body of man. It was further revealed to him that the Holy Ghost is a personage of Spirit, distinct and separate from the personali-ties of the Father and the Son. This all-important truth staggered the world. . . .

Joseph Smith beheld the Father and the Son; therefore he could testify with personal knowledge that the scriptures were true wherein we read: "So God created man in his own image, in the image of God created he him; male and female created he them." This was to be understood literally, and not in some mys-tical or figurative sense.

In the year 1820, the universal doctrine in the so-called Christian world was that the canon of scripture is full, that the heavens were closed against further revelation, and that it was folly to look for more. Joseph Smith's vision contradicted all this, for he saw the heavens opened and was ministered to by heav-enly messengers sent from the Lord. Who was right, Joseph Smith or the teachers of men? Amos said: "Surely the Lord God will do nothing, but he revealeth his secret unto his servants the prophets" (Amos 3:7). . . . Again we find Joseph Smith in har-mony with the Bible truth. . . .

When we stop to consider that the Prophet Joseph Smith was but fourteen years of age when his first announcement of revela-tion from the heavens was declared, and that his ministry covered the brief space of only fourteen years from the organization of the Church until his martyrdom, at the age of thirty-eight years, what he accomplished for the salvation of man is wonderful to behold. He was not trained in the schools of his time, and he was considered by his enemies to be an unlearned man; yet, in the light of his life's labors we are forced to say indeed that what he did has proved to be "a marvelous work and a wonder." Thus through the weak things of the world have come forth strength and power which have broken down the mighty and the strong ones, whose wisdom has perished and whose understanding has been hid. (*Improvement Era*, Apr. 1920, 496–498, 504.)

The Lord, in the former dispensation, sent a messenger to prepare the way before him, and in this dispensation it was just as necessary that a messenger be sent to prepare the way for the coming of the Lord and the establishment of the reign of peace. If Joseph Smith was not that man, then we must look for another. Now, I say to you, the issue is clear, the line is sharply drawn and there is no occasion for misunderstanding. Either Joseph Smith was a prophet of God, and all that he claimed to be, or he was the greatest impostor this world has ever seen. There is no middle ground. You cannot say he was deceived, that he was mistaken, that he believed that he was called of God and thought that he had seen a vision of the Father and the Son but he was in error. He was all he claimed to be, or else he was a base deceiver. . . . There is no possibility of his being deceived, and on this issue we are ready to make our stand. I maintain that Joseph Smith was all that he claimed to be. His statements are too positive and his claims too great to admit of deception on his part. No impostor could have accomplished so great and wonderful a work. (Conference Report, Apr. 1920, 106.)

There is no account in history or revelation extant, where ever before both the Father and the Son appeared in the presence of mortal man in glory. Most wonderful was the honor bestowed upon this unsophisticated boy. Great was his faith—so great that he was able, like the brother of Jared, to penetrate the veil and behold the glory of these holy Beings, whose glory rested upon him. Without this power overshadowing him, he could not have endured their presence, for their brightness was far greater than the brightness of the noonday sun. It was not, therefore, with the power of the natural eye that this great Vision was beheld, but by the aid of the eye of the spirit. The natural man, without the saving grace of the power of the Lord, could not behold his presence in this manner, for he would be consumed. Joseph Smith, through the power of the Lord, was able to behold the presence of the Great Creator and his Glorified Son, for they deigned to honor him with their presence and converse with him.

No longer were the heavens as brass. No more would man be forced to stumble and grope in darkness. Salvation was made known and the glad tidings were to sound forth, as with the blast of a mighty trumpet, to the ends of the earth. Satan's reign was nearing its end, and the message of eternal peace was shortly to be proclaimed to every nation, and kindred, and tongue and people.

No wonder Joseph Smith rejoiced, he now possessed greater knowledge than all the professors and divines in all the world! . . . But great disappointment awaited him, for with one accord his message was rejected. Only the members of his household would believe. He was treated with scorn by great men of learning, although he was but a boy. He was mocked and shamed. Instead of the spirit of love and gratefulness following him for revealing this glorious message of truth, it was the spirit of contempt and hatred with which he had to contend. In sorrow he learned to hold his peace and wait—wait for further light and inspiration which he had been promised. Though all the world should mock and former friends deride, he knew he had beheld the Vision. There was one Friend to whom he now could go and pour out his soul in humble hope of encouragement and succor. What did it matter though the whole world should laugh, if the Son of God would hearken to his humble pleadings?

Yet, when we stop to reflect, it is not strange that this message of light and truth should be rejected by the world, for the Lord had said long years before, "Men love darkness rather than light, because their deeds are evil." As for the priests, was not their craft in danger? . . . The Vision had shattered the traditions of the times. The doctrines taught in the churches were emphatically contradicted and disproved. The world was teaching and believing that the canon of scripture was full; that there was not to be and could not be, more revelation; that the visitation of angels had ceased with the early Christian fathers, and such things as these had passed away forever. Again, the doctrine was taught that the Father, Son and Holy Ghost were incomprehensible, without body, parts and passions. A revelation of the Father and the Son as separate persons, each with a body tangible and in the form of the body of man, was destructive of this doctrine, as revelation was of the doctrine of the closed heavens. . . .

A bold denunciation of all such false teachings and traditions, although told in confiding simplicity by a humble youth, fourteen years of age, was not likely to bring rejoicing and peace of mind to those who thus believed and loved their old traditions dearly. Nevertheless the story must be told; for in the world were thousands of honest souls who were likewise praying that the light of the everlasting Gospel would be restored, and the message of salvation again be proclaimed as a witness before the end of unrighteousness should come. (Smith, *Essentials in Church History* [1922], 41, 46–47.)

I have answered the question as to why the Father introduced the Son, and why it was the Son who spoke to Joseph Smith, because all revelations since the day of Adam's casting out of the Garden of Eden have come through Jesus Christ. . . .

If the Prophet was telling a falsehood when he went into the woods to pray, he never would have come out and said that he had seen a vision of the Father and the Son and that they were separate Personages, and that the Father introduced the Son and then told the Prophet to address his question to the Son, who would give him the answer. The Prophet never would have thought of such a thing as that, had it been a fraud.

If he had come out of the woods saying he had seen a vision, had it been untrue never would he have thought of separating

Father and Son, nor would he have ever thought of having the Father introduce the Son and for him to put his question to the Son to receive his answer. He never could have thought of it; for that was the farthest thing from the ideas existing in the world in the year 1820. (Conference Report, Apr. 1960, 71–72.)

Harold B. Lee

Harold B. Lee (1899–1973) was called to be an apostle in 1941 and became church president in 1972. Earlier, he had been the architect of the Church welfare program and one of the key creators of the Church correlation program.

A theophany [is] an experience where the Father or the Son or both put in a personal appearance, or speak directly to man. Moses talked with the Lord face to face; Daniel had a theophany, or personal appearance. . . . At the conversion of Paul, there was also a personal appearance, and an audible voice was heard. . . .

Perhaps the greatest of all theophanies of our time was the appearance of the Father and the Son to the Prophet Joseph Smith in the grove. (*Teachings of the Presidents of the Church: Harold B. Lee* [2000], 50.)

Spencer W. Kimball

Spencer W. Kimball (1895–1985) was a grandson of apostle Heber C. Kimball, who served with both Joseph Smith and Brigham Young. Spencer Kimball was called to be an apostle in 1943 and began service as Church president in 1973.

One young man in his early teens lacked wisdom but was not lacking in faith or sincerity. His prayer opened a closed heaven and a confused world for further exploration. The common woods were made sacred that day; they blazed in glory. The trees were hallowed and the soil made holy ground. (*BYU Speeches*, 11 Oct. 1961, 3.)

Under special need, at special times, under proper circumstances, God reveals himself to men who are prepared for such manifestations. And since God is the same yesterday, today, and forever, the heavens cannot be closed except as men lock them against themselves with disbelief.

In our own dispensation came [such a] grand experience. The need was imperative; an apostasy had covered the earth and gross darkness the people, and the minds of men were clouded and light had been obscured in darkness. The time had come. Religious liberty would protect the seed until it could germinate and grow. And the individual was prepared in the person of a youth, clean and open minded, who had such implicit faith in the response of God that the heavens could not remain as iron and the earth as brass as they had been for many centuries.

This budding prophet had no preconceived false notions and beliefs. He was not steeped in the traditions and legends and superstitions and fables of the centuries. He had nothing to unlearn. He prayed for knowledge and direction. The powers of darkness preceded the light. When he knelt in solitude in the silent forest, his earnest prayer brought on a battle royal that threatened his destruction. . . . Young Joseph finally recovered his voice and asked the pertinent questions for which he had come and a conversation ensued, most of which was forbidden him to write. . . .

Joseph had had the same general experience of Abraham and Moses and Enoch who had seen the Lord and heard his voice. In addition, he heard the Father, bearing witness of the Son, as had Peter, James, and John on Transfiguration's Mount. He had seen the person of Elohim. He had fought a desperate battle with the powers of darkness as had Moses and Abraham. And like them all, he was protected by the glory of the Lord. This young man gave a new concept to the world. Now at least one person knew God without question, for he had seen and heard. (Conference Report, Apr. 1964, 97–98.)

Nothing short of this total vision to Joseph could have served the purpose to clear away the mists of the centuries. Merely an impression, a hidden voice, a dream could [not] have dispelled the old vagaries and misconceptions of the ages. (*Improvement Era*, Dec. 1966, 1106.)

Of all the great events of the century, none compared with the first vision of Joseph Smith. . . .

He had now seen heavenly messengers, the Father of all who introduced THE SON, Jesus Christ. He had met divine royalty. Never before in hundreds of years had such a spectacular, meaningful vision burst upon a human being. The God of all these worlds and the Son of God, the Redeemer, our Savior, in person, attended this boy. He saw the living God. He saw the living Christ. . . .

Unspeakable things Joseph heard which he could neither write nor speak, like the three on the Mount of Transfiguration, when the same Lord charged them "Tell the vision to no man." . . .

A new world has come into view. An iron ceiling has burst asunder—the heavens are open, communication is again continuous between heaven and earth.

. . . For eighteen centuries, nothing has ever happened to compare with this in breadth and length and depth. The sun is risen and the darkness of ages dissipated. . . .

This young boy was entrusted with the greatest block of knowledge known to men. Remember, that spring morning not one of all the people in the world had *absolute knowledge of God.* There were many good people, but they had all walked in spiritual darkness these many centuries. But *here was a boy who knew.* . . .

Joseph *knew,* as no other soul living, these absolutes:

He knew that God lives, that He is a [glorified] person with flesh and bones and personality, like us or we like Him, in His image. . . .

He knew . . . knew that the Father and the Son were two distinct beings with form, voices, and . . . personalities.

He knew that the gospel was not on the earth, . . . for the God of heaven and earth had so informed him. . . .

Joseph *knew* from firsthand experience the attributes of the Father and the Son and the program that was to be restored through him. (Speech, Logan Utah Institute, 13 Dec. 1970, 1, 6, 7.)

The heavens which had been closed in large measure for many centuries were now opened. . . . The revelation that had been well-nigh obliterated and reasoned out of existence was again available. . . .

In that moment there was only one man on the face of the whole earth who knew with absolute assurance that God was a personal being, that the Father and Son were separate individuals with [glorified] bodies of flesh and bones [and that he] had been created in their image. . . .

That morning in the grove in New York when the Father and Son came to him was perhaps the greatest revelation ever given to the world. (*Teachings of Presidents of the Church: Spencer W. Kimball* [2011], 230.)

I bear witness to the world today that more than a century and a half ago the iron ceiling was shattered; the heavens were once again opened, and since that time revelations have been continuous.

That new day dawned when [a] soul with passionate yearning prayed for divine guidance. A spot of hidden solitude was found, knees were bent, a heart was humbled, pleadings were voiced, and a light brighter than the noonday sun illuminated the world—the curtain never to be closed again.

A young lad . . . , Joseph Smith, of incomparable faith, broke the spell, shattered the "heavens of iron" and reestablished communication. Heaven kissed the earth, light dissipated the darkness, and God again spoke to man. . . . A new prophet was in the land and through him God set up his kingdom, never to be destroyed nor left to another people—a kingdom that will stand forever. (*Ensign*, May 1977, 77–78.)

Ezra Taft Benson

Ezra Taft Benson (1855–1994) was a great-grandson of apostle Ezra T. Benson. Elder Benson was called as an apostle in 1943 and began service as Church president in 1985. He also served in the cabinet of U.S. president Dwight D. Eisenhower from 1952 to 1961.

The first vision of the Prophet Joseph Smith is bedrock theology to the Church. The adversary knows this and has attacked Joseph Smith's credibility from the day he announced the visitation of the Father and the Son. You should always bear testimony to the truth of the First Vision. Joseph Smith did see the Father and the Son. They conversed with him as he said they did. . . . If we do not accept this truth—if we have not received a witness about this great revelation—we cannot inspire faith in those whom we lead. (*Teachings of Ezra Taft Benson* [1988], 101.)

Howard W. Hunter

Howard W. Hunter (1907–1995) was an attorney who was called to be an apostle in 1959. He became the fourteenth president of the Church in 1994 but died the following year.

I am grateful for my membership in the Church; and my testimony of its divinity hinges upon the simple story of the lad under the trees kneeling and receiving heavenly visitors— not one God, but two separate, individual personages, the Father and the Son, revealing again to the earth the personages of the Godhead. My faith and testimony hinge upon this simple story, for if it is not true, Mormonism falls. If it is true—and I bear witness that it is—it is one of the greatest single events in all history. . . .

I think there is no more beautiful story in all of history than the simple, sweet story of the lad who went into the woods near his home, kneeling in prayer and receiving heavenly visitors. (Speech, Logan Utah Institute, 1960.)

In the year 1820 the silence was broken, and the Lord again appeared to a prophet. This prophet, Joseph Smith, could testify of his own positive knowledge that God lives, that Jesus is the Christ, the Son of God, a Resurrected Being, separate and distinct from the Father. He did not testify as to what he believed or what he or others thought or conjectured, but of what he knew. This knowledge came to him because God the Father and the Son appeared to him in person and spoke to him. (Conference Report, Oct. 1963, 100–101.)

Joseph Smith was not only a great man, but he was an inspired servant of the Lord, a prophet of God. His greatness consists in one thing—the truthfulness of his declaration that he saw the Father and the Son and that he responded to the reality of that divine revelation. . . .

For the first time in eighteen hundred years, God had revealed himself as a personal being. Furthermore, the Father and the Son demonstrated the undeniable truth that they are separate and distinct personages. Indeed, the relationship of the Father and the Son was reaffirmed by the divine introduction to the boy prophet, "This is My Beloved Son. Hear Him." (JS—H 1:17.) . . .

I testify . . . that the Father and the Son did appear to the Prophet Joseph Smith to initiate this great rolling forth of the latter-day work in our time. (*Ensign*, May 1991, 64.)

Gordon B. Hinckley

Gordon B. Hinckley (1910–2008) was a nephew of apostle Alonzo A. Hinckley. He authored several books, including a short history of the Church, Truth Restored. *He was called to be an apostle in 1961, served as counselor in the First Presidency to three presidents, and became president of the Church in 1995.*

In establishing and opening this dispensation our Father did so with a revelation of himself and of his Son Jesus Christ, as if to say to all the world that he was weary of the attempts of men, earnest though these attempts might have been, to define and describe him. Strange as it seems, we alone, among all the great organizations that worship God, have a true description and a true definition of him.

The experience of Joseph Smith in a few moments in the grove on a spring day in 1820, brought more light and knowledge and understanding of the personality and reality and substance of God and his Beloved Son than men had arrived at during centuries of speculation. (Conference Report, Apr. 1960, 82–83.)

[The First Vision] opened the marvelous work of restoration. It lifted the curtain on the long-promised dispensation of the fullness of times.

For more than a century and a half, enemies, critics, and some would-be scholars have worn out their lives trying to disprove the validity of that vision. Of course they cannot understand it. The things of God are understood by the Spirit of God. There had been nothing of comparable magnitude since the Son of God walked the earth in mortality. Without it as a foundation stone for our faith and organization, we have nothing. With it, we have everything. (*Ensign,* Nov. 1984, 53.)

Much has been written, much will be written, in an effort to explain [the First Vision] away. The finite mind cannot comprehend it. But the testimony of the Holy Spirit, experienced by countless numbers of people all through the years since it happened, bears witness that it is true, that it happened as Joseph Smith said it happened, that it was as real as the sunrise over Palmyra, that it is an essential foundation stone, a cornerstone, without which the Church could not be "fitly framed together." (Conference Report, Oct. 1984, 68.)

I add my testimony that Joseph was and is the great prophet of this dispensation of the fulness of times, that he was raised up by the God of heaven, that he was tutored and directed by the risen Lord Jesus Christ and also by angels who were sent from the heavens to restore the everlasting priesthood with all of its powers and keys to reestablish the Church of Jesus Christ in the earth and to set in motion a cause and kingdom that will spread to every nation, kindred, tongue, and people. (*BYU Speeches,* 3 Sept. 1989, 15.)

[Joseph Smith] brought us a true knowledge of God, the Eternal Father, and His Risen Son, the Lord Jesus Christ. During the short time of his great vision he learned more concerning the nature of Deity than all of those who through centuries had argued the matter in learned councils and scholarly forums. (*Ensign,* Dec. 1997, 2.)

Our entire case as members of The Church of Jesus Christ of Latter-day Saints rest on the validity of [the] glorious First Vision. It was the parting of the curtain to open this, the dispensation of the fullness of times. Nothing on which we base our doctrine, nothing we teach, nothing we live by is of greater importance than this initial declaration. I submit that if Joseph Smith talked with God the Father and His Beloved Son, then all else of which he spoke is true. This is the hinge on which turns the gate that leads to the path of salvation and eternal life. (*Ensign,* Nov. 1998, 71.)

We declare without equivocation that God the Father and His Son, the Lord Jesus Christ, appeared in person to the boy Joseph Smith. . . .

Our whole strength rests on the validity of that vision. It either occurred or it did not occur. If it did not, then this work is a fraud. If it's true, it's the most important and wonderful work under the heavens. . . .

Upon that unique and wonderful experience stands the validity of this Church.

In all of recorded religious history there is nothing to compare with it. . . .

It is easy to see why people do not accept this account. It is almost beyond comprehension. And yet it is so reasonable. . . .

That They came, both of Them, that Joseph saw Them in Their resplendent glory, that They spoke to him and that he heard and recorded Their words—of these remarkable things we testify. . . .

The truth of that unique, singular, and remarkable event is the pivotal substance of our faith. . . .

We testify that the heavens have been opened, that the curtains have been parted, that God has spoken, and that Jesus Christ has manifested Himself, followed by a bestowal of divine authority. (*Ensign,* Nov. 2002, 80–81.)

How deeply grateful I am that we of this Church do not rely on any man-made statement concerning the nature of Deity. Our knowledge comes directly from the personal experience of Joseph Smith, who, while yet a boy, spoke with God the Eternal Father and His Beloved Son, the Risen Lord. He knelt in Their presence; he heard Their voices; and he responded. Each was a distinct personality. Small wonder that he told his mother that he had learned that her church was not true. And so, one of the great over-arching doctrines of this Church is our belief in God the Eternal Father. He is a being, real and individual. He is the great Governor of the universe, yet He is our Father, and we are His children. (*Ensign,* May 2007, 83.)

Thomas S. Monson

Thomas S. Monson (1927–2018) was called to be an apostle in 1963, at the young age of thirty-six. He served as counselor to two Church presidents and became president himself in 2008.

When but fourteen years of age, this courageous young man [Joseph Smith] entered a grove of trees, which later would be called sacred, and received an answer to his sincere prayer. There followed for Joseph unrelenting persecution as he related to others the account of the glorious vision he received in that grove. Yet, although he was ridiculed and scorned, he stood firm. Said he, "I had seen a vision; I knew it, and I knew that God knew it, and I could not deny it, neither dared I do it" (Joseph Smith–History 1:25). Step by step, facing opposition at nearly every turn and yet always guided by the hand of the Lord, Joseph organized The Church of Jesus Christ of Latter-day Saints. He proved courageous in all that he did. (*Ensign*, Nov. 2002, 62.)

Russell M. Nelson

Russell M. Nelson (1924–present) was a world-renowned heart surgeon. He was called to be an apostle in 1984 and Church president in 2018.

How can we become the men and women—the Christlike servants—the Lord needs us to be? How can we find answers to questions that perplex us? If Joseph Smith's transcendent experience in the Sacred Grove teaches us anything, it is that the heavens are open and that God speaks to His children.

The Prophet Joseph Smith set a pattern for us to follow in resolving our questions. Drawn to the promise of James that if we lack wisdom we may ask of God, the boy Joseph took his question directly to Heavenly Father. He sought personal revelation, and his seeking opened this last dispensation. (*Ensign*, May 2018, 95.)

Apostles

(arranged in order of their call)

Anthon H. Lund

Anthon H. Lund (1844–1921) became an apostle under John Taylor and later served in two First Presidencies.

This Spring it will be one hundred years since an event happened which was epoch-making in the faith of many thousands of people. This event took place in the Spring of 1820. A young boy, but little past fourteen years of age, was deeply concerned in regard to choosing the right church that taught the true principles of the gospel of Jesus Christ.

This anxiety was caused by the great excitement that existed at that time in his neighborhood concerning religion. Each of the different denominations was claiming that its mode of worship was the only correct one, and that its members had the true gospel. As the teachings of each one of the sects were far from being in harmony with those of the others—in fact, contrary to them—the young boy was bewildered. He thought there could be only one accepted of God. . . .

The important question to him was, Which sect has the true Gospel? He was a firm believer in the Bible, and he sought in this divine storehouse of truth, to find a solution. He read what James writes in the first chapter and fifth verse of his letter: "If any of you lack wisdom, let him ask of God, that giveth to all men liberally, and upbraideth not; and it shall be given him." The young man felt that he was greatly in need of wisdom, and that in this passage a disciple of Christ had given him a key to obtain the knowledge for which he hungered. He had full faith in the words of the inspired writer, and concluded to follow his instruction.

A short distance west of his father's house there is a small grove, which, from that which occurred there, has been called the Sacred Grove. We do not know the exact date, when the future prophet offered the prayer that opened the heavens, which had for so long a time seemed to be of brass; but he says it was in the Spring. He was seeking solitude, and as he had not prayed before, using his own words, he was, no doubt, shy to let any one know what he intended to do, or to see him kneeling, and the solitude he sought would not be obtained while the trees were bare; so, I would judge that the trees were clothed in their fresh, verdant attire; hence, some time in late April. . . .

No doubt the adversary of mankind did not desire that this young person should learn the pitiful conditions of the world in regard to the true knowledge of God, and, therefore, did all to crush him, but help was near, and the enemy fled. . . .

Hearing the precious words: *"This is my beloved Son, hear him,"* made plain to young Joseph that the Speaker was God, our heavenly Father; and that the other personage was Jesus Christ, the Son of God. . . .

That which Joseph Smith saw and heard in his first Vision is contrary to the belief of the Christian world; and that which seems to us to be of the greatest importance is wholly denied by professors of religion. We will examine these points. . . . To make them clear to our minds, we will limit them to three propositions, or questions:

I. Has God a body, parts, and passions, and was man created in his image?

II. Has there been a general apostasy, and have professors of religion taught for doctrines commandments of men?

III. Is belief in new revelation false?

I. That God has neither body, parts, nor passions is the general belief of the Christian world; but it seems to us that the Bible is very clear to the contrary in its statements concerning God, for it teaches that man was created in his likeness. "And God said let us make man in our image, after our likeness." "So God created man in his own image, in the image of God created he him; male and female created he them." The young boy Joseph saw that man was indeed created in the image and likeness of God, and that the doctrine denying this was a doctrine devised by man. . . .

II. The Personage who spoke to Joseph told him not to join any of the sects; for they were all wrong.

From this we infer that the true gospel was not on the earth. . . . The prophetic writers foresaw that such a condition would exist. In Paul's second letter to the Thessalonians, second chapter and first verse, he writes: "Now we beseech you, brethren, by the coming of our Lord Jesus Christ, and by our gathering together unto him, that ye be not soon shaken in mind, or be troubled, neither by spirit, nor by word, nor by letter as from us, as that the day of Christ is at hand. Let no man deceive you by any means; for that day shall not come, except there come a falling away first, and that man of sin be revealed, the son of perdition; who opposeth and exalteth himself above all that is called God, or that is worshiped; so that he as God sitteth in the temple of God, showing himself that he is God." . . .

No wonder that the testimony of young Joseph stirred up the professors of religion against Joseph, but he dared not deny or smooth down that which he had heard. . . .

III. Is belief in new revelation false? That God will not reveal himself in our age is generally held by the religious denominations. Joseph, the young boy, having implicit faith in the word of God, proved the words of James were true. His prayer was heard; the Father and the Son appeared unto him. He saw them descending from heaven. They instructed him not to join any of the sects, because they were all wrong. He was astonished to find that when he told what he had seen and heard he was persecuted. He says: "Why persecute me for telling the truth? I have actually seen a vision, and who am I that I can withstand God, or does the world think to make me deny what I have actually seen? For I had seen a vision; I knew it, and I knew that God knew it, and I could not deny it, neither dared I do it, at least I knew that by so doing I would offend God, and come under condemnation."

After this first vision he received many other revelations for the guidance of the Church. He was informed that this is the "dispensation of the fulness of times." As all other dispensations had been introduced by revelation from God, so also this was ushered in by heavenly beings revealing the mind and will of God to men. . . .

In studying the first vision of Joseph and what he saw and heard, the Scriptures, history, and the fulfilment of the words of revelations received afterwards, all bear witness to the truthfulness of the young man and of the truths he enunciated. (*Improvement Era*, Apr. 1920, 475–483.)

Rudger Clawson

Rudger Clawson (1857–1943) was called to be an apostle by Lorenzo Snow. He served for forty-five years, half of which was as president of the Quorum of the Twelve.

[In] the Pearl of Great Price, . . . you will further find a narration by the Prophet himself of the First Vision. . . . He gives an account of it in simple and impressive language. It is beautiful; the very simplicity of it is beautiful indeed. That communication did not come to us in scientific terms. No, it does not need to be translated. A child can understand the story of that First Vision, it is so simple and beautiful. (Conference Report, Apr. 1920, 65.)

Charles W. Penrose

Charles W. Penrose (1832–1925) was called to be an apostle under Joseph F. Smith and served in two First Presidencies.

In the early spring of the year 1820 there occurred something unique in the annals of time. The Almighty God, Creator of heaven and earth, architect of the universe, center of life and light, with his beloved Son, the immortal Christ, the world's Redeemer, in the brightness of their glory, casting into shade the morning sunbeams of that beautiful day, manifested themselves to humble, trembling humanity. Not amid the thunderings of disturbed elements, in flame of fire or frowning cloud, in quaking earth or acclaiming heavenly hosts, to gaping crowds or proud professors or learned divines, but in a quiet grove near an obscure village of a sparsely populated part of western New York state, and to a mere boy, little over fourteen years of age, of the common names—Joseph and Smith, who knelt in earnest faith and prayer seeking to know which of all the clanging "Christian" sects had the true religion.

The story of this great revelation has been published far and wide but has never been told with greater effect than as given in simple form by the boy Prophet himself. The substance of it is that on beholding the two glorious beings he asked the momentous question; and one of them pointing to the other replied: *"This is my beloved Son, hear him."*

The boy then received, through the Son, the information that the entire religious world was astray, and the injunction to go after none of the sects, for their teachings were but "the commandments of men." He was promised that in due time the fulness of the everlasting gospel should be made known to him.

This was something new indeed. Not only to the opening, remarkable century, but to all the preceding ages. Never before, so far as history has recorded, was Deity thus fully manifested. The Father and the Son as distinct and separate personalities, spiritual, but tangible beings in human form, the Holy Spirit emanating from them as light and life and witness of their divinity to the soul of the inspired youth seeking after God! No mere immaterial, bodiless, incomprehensible abstractions were they or either of them, but real, actual beings, with form and feature and individuality, the Father and His Son each in the majesty and unity of exalted, perfected, and glorified humanity. The great truth was made plain that God did literally make man "in his own likeness" and that Christ Jesus was "the express image of his person."

Another great fact set forth was the utter departure of the whole world from the true Christian faith and worship, with the truth that "God is not the author of confusion" or contention or discord, as manifest throughout entire Christendom. The complete lack of Divine authority was also disclosed, showing that all administrations of ordinances in the name of the Holy Trinity were void and of no heavenly effect. The absolute need of a new divine dispensation was thus made palpable.

That wondrous vision was the opening scene of the great latter-day glory and "restitution of all things" predicted by the holy prophets. (*Improvement Era*, Apr. 1920, 484–487.)

Orson F. Whitney

Orson F. Whitney (1855–1931) was a grandson of Newel K. Whitney and Heber C. Kimball. He was called to be an apostle in 1906 by Joseph F. Smith.

Joseph Smith did not give us anything new; he brought back the old; old things are best. The eternal truth of God must be old, it cannot be new for it never had a beginning, it will never have an end. That is the first thing that Joseph Smith did for the world: To restore this precious knowledge of the true God. And, it is a little singular and yet it is very beautiful to me, that when Joseph went into the woods to ask in his simple manner which of all the Christian churches was the true Church, God gave him a greater answer than he was looking for. Joseph wanted to know which of all the churches was the true church. It had never dawned upon this boy's mind but that one of them was right, and he was told that none of them was right, that they had all gone out of the way; that they were teaching for doctrine the commandments of man, and that God was about to restore the gospel to the earth again and that he had a mission in connection therewith. But that was not the greatest part of that wonderful revelation. The greatest part is the part that He did not speak. The boy saw two beings before him – two glorious beings in the form of man and, before a word had been uttered that great truth had been restored that God is indeed what Moses said, in the form and image of man, and one of these glorious Beings said of the other: "this is my beloved son, hear Him." The inference is therefore that the one who spoke first was our Father in heaven who had come down to open this new dispensation for the love of His children, and had brought with Him the Savior who had come down to open this new dispensation for the love of His children, and had brought with Him the Savior who had died that His children might live. We can approach with confidence such a God, who notes the sparrow's fall, and knows that there is no man, no woman, no human soul so little, so insignificant but God has a care over them and desires to bless them and save them. (Discourse, Ogden, Utah Weber North Stake, 25 June 1916, LDS Church History Library.)

Joseph Smith's first great service to humanity was in bringing back the lost knowledge of the true and living God. . . . It devolved upon Joseph Smith to shatter the false doctrine of a bodiless, passionless Deity, and bring back the precious knowledge that had been lost. . . .

We are all familiar with the story—how a boy of fourteen years went into the forest and prayed; how he wrestled with Satan, and was delivered; how he saw a light above his head brighter than the noonday sun, and in the midst of it two glorious beings in the form of man, One of whom, pointing to the Other, said: "This is my beloved Son, hear him." From that hour, there was one person, at least, upon this planet who knew what kind of a being God is. . . . It was no accident, no chance happening—Joseph Smith's going into the grove that spring morning, one hundred years ago. It was an event predestined, heaven-inspired. . . .

It was no ordinary man that went into the woods that morning to pray. It was a Prophet, a Seer. Joseph Smith was not made a prophet by the people who held up their hands for him on the sixth of April, 1830, when this Church was organized. He was already a prophet, chosen, as Abraham had been, before he was born; ordained, like Jeremiah, before he was formed in the flesh. The people merely "sustained" him in that position, manifesting by the uplifted hand that they were willing to follow him as their leader, and' to accept of his ministrations in that capacity. He was already a prophet, already a seer; God had made him such in advance. But all men are not Joseph Smiths. He was a man like unto Moses. He was the rarest human being that has walked this earth in the past two thousand years. And why did he go into the grove that morning and pray for wisdom and light? It was because the time had come. The Hour had struck, and The Man was there—the man whom God had provided. (Conference Report, Apr. 1920, 122–123.)

James E. Talmage

James E. Talmage (1862–1933) was a scientist, professor at Brigham Young Academy and University of Utah, president of University of Utah, and the author of two classic books, Jesus the Christ *and* Articles of Faith, *which still remain in print. He was called to be an apostle in 1911.*

In reading the earliest pages of "Mormon" history, we are introduced to a man whose name will ever be prominent in the story of the Church—the founder of the organization by common usage of the term, the head of the system as an earthly establishment—one who is accepted by the Church as an ambassador specially commissioned of God to be the first revelator of the latter-day dispensation. This man is Joseph Smith, commonly known as the "Mormon" prophet. Rarely indeed does history present an organization, religious, social, or political, in which an individual holds as conspicuous and in all ways as important a place as does this man in the development of "Mormonism." . . .

Joseph Smith was born at Sharon, Vermont, in December, 1805. He was the son of industrious parents, who possessed strong religious tendencies and tolerant natures. For generations his ancestors had been laborers, by occupation tillers of the soil; and though comfortable circumstances had generally been their lot, reverses and losses in the father's house had brought the family to poverty; so that from his earliest days the lad Joseph was made acquainted with the pleasures and pains of hard work. He is described as having been more than ordinarily studious for his years; and when that powerful wave of religious agitation and sectarian revival which characterized the first quarter of the last century, reached the home of the Smiths, Joseph with others of the family was profoundly affected. The household became somewhat divided on the subject of religion, . . . but Joseph, while favorably impressed by the Methodists in comparison with others, confesses that his mind was sorely troubled over the contemplation of the strife and tumult existing among the religious bodies; and he hesitated. He tried in vain to solve the mystery presented to him in the warring factions of what professed to be the Church of Christ. Surely, thought he, these several churches, opposed as they are to one another on what appear to be the vital points of religion, cannot all be right. While puzzling over this anomaly he chanced upon this verse in the epistle of James [1:5.] . . .

In common with so many others, the earnest youth found here within the scriptures, admonition and counsel as directly applicable to his case and circumstances as if the lines had been addressed to him by name. A brief period of hesitation, in which he shrank from the thought that a mortal like himself, weak, youthful, and unlearned, should approach the Creator with a personal request, was followed by a humble and contrite resolution to act upon the counsel of the ancient apostle. The result, to which he bore solemn record (testifying at first with the simplicity and enthusiasm of youth, afterward confirming the declaration with manhood's increasing powers, and at last voluntarily sealing the testimony with his life's blood,) proved most startling to the sectarian world—a world in which according to popular belief no new revelation of truth was possible. It is a surprising fact that while growth, progress, advancement, development of known truths and the acquisition of new ones, characterize every living science, the sectarian world has declared that nothing new must be expected as direct revelation from God.

The testimony of this lad is, that in response to his supplication, drawn forth by the admonition of an inspired apostle, he received a divine ministration; heavenly beings manifested themselves to him—two, clothed in purity, and alike in form and feature. Pointing to the other, one said, "This is my beloved Son, hear Him." In answer to the lad's prayer, the heavenly personage so designated informed Joseph that the Spirit of God dwelt not with warring sects, which, while professing a form of godliness, denied the power thereof, and that he should join none of them. Overjoyed at the glorious manifestation thus granted unto him, the boy prophet could not withhold from relatives and acquaintances tidings of the heavenly vision. From the ministers, who had been so energetic in their efforts to convert the boy, he received, to his surprise, abuse and ridicule. "Visions and manifestations from God," said they, "are of the past, and all such things ceased with the apostles of old; the canon of scripture is full; religion has reached its perfection in plan, and, unlike all other systems contrived or accepted by human kind, is incapable of development or growth. It is true God lives, but He cares not for His children of modern times as He did for those of ancient days; He has shut Himself away from the people, closed the windows of heaven, and has suspended all direct communication with the people of earth."

. . . The importance of this alleged revelation from the heavens to the earth is such as to demand attentive consideration. If a fact, it is a full contradiction of the vague theories that had been increasing and accumulating for centuries, denying personality and parts to Deity.

In 1820, there lived one person who knew that the word of the Creator, "Let us make man in our own image, after our likeness," had a meaning more than in metaphor. Joseph Smith, the youthful prophet and revelator of the nineteenth century, knew that the Eternal Father and the well-beloved Son, Jesus Christ, were in form and stature like unto perfect men; and that the human family was in very truth of divine origin. (Talmage, *The Story of Mormonism* [1907], 3–9.)

The spring of 1820 stands recorded as a time of transcendent import in the chronicles of both heaven and earth. For many centuries the human mind, heart, and soul, had been beclouded by false precept and darkening dogma respecting Deity. Through apostasy and its inseparable ignorance mankind had actually lost the knowledge of God. This dire condition had been foreseen and predicted by holy prophets, apostles and seers, and by the Lord Christ himself.

By human search alone man cannot find God. The knowledge of Deity and Divine attributes once lost by the race can never be recovered save through a new revelation from the heavens.

When, at the season named, the pure-hearted, truth-seeking lad, Joseph Smith, sought seclusion in the grove to pray for guidance in a matter that he considered of vital importance to his soul, he moved to action the supreme powers of both good and evil.

Evil first vented its rage upon the youthful suppliant, he was buffeted by Satanic fury, and all the agencies of darkness conspired to terrify and deter. Feeling that without the intervention of a mightier power he would be utterly destroyed, he called all the more earnestly upon God for aid. Let the lad's own words tell the wondrous story:

"Just at this moment of great alarm, I saw a pillar of light exactly over my head, above the brightness of the sun, which descended gradually until it fell upon me.

"It no sooner appeared than I found myself delivered from the enemy which held me bound. When the light rested upon me I saw two Personages, whose brightness and glory defy all description, standing above me in the air. One of them spake unto me, calling me by name, and said, pointing to the other — *This is my beloved Son. Hear Him.*"

The question about which Joseph had been most troubled, and for answer to which he had sought the Lord in obedience to scriptural precept and promise (see James 1:5), was as to which of all the contending sects and churches of the time was the Church of Christ. The Beloved Son, Jesus the Christ, instructed him to refrain from joining any of the sects, as their teachings were the precepts of men, at best but a form of godliness devoid of the power thereof.

The Scriptures extant hold no record of a theophany, or personal manifestation of Deity, so glorious as was this. On three earlier occasions, each marking the inauguration of a distinctive dispensation of Divine purpose and authority, had the Voice of the Eternal Father been heard, attesting the Godship of Jesus Christ. These were severally:

(1) At the time of our Lord's baptism in Jordan.

(2) At His transfiguration.

(3) When, as a resurrected and glorified Being, He ministered to the descendants of Lehi on the American continent.

In all these manifestations, the Father was heard but not seen, so far as Sacred Writ avers. In the latest attestation of the Son's authority by the Father the Two stood side by side.

It is consistent with the distinguishing supremacy of the Last Dispensation—the Dispensation of Fulness—into which all authority and powers of earlier dispensations are to be gathered and restored, that its beginning should be signalized by Divine disclosures of surpassing purport and significance.

The appearing of the Eternal Father and His Son Jesus Christ to Joseph Smith, in the spring of 1820, marked the end of a long era of apostasy and ignorance, except as unbelief or sin yet enthralls the individual soul.

Through that transcendent event, the knowledge of the personality of both Father and Son was again given to man.

The plain and ennobling truth that God is literally in the physical form and image after which man has been created was established anew.

Thereby, also, was the fact reaffirmed that in His dealings with the human race the Father operates through Jesus Christ the Son. "Hear Him" was the Father's commandment to Joseph, and through Joseph to the world. In harmony therewith stands the testimony of Christ given of old: "I am the way, the truth, and the life: no man cometh unto the Father, but by me" (John 14:6).

The theophany of 1820 demonstrated that the Church of Christ was not existent upon earth, and furthermore that for its reestablishment a special delegation of power and appointment was requisite.

It marked the ushering in of the Dispensation of the Fulness of Times, of which the olden prophets had spoken, and which shall continue until the Lord Jesus Christ returns to earth to inaugurate the Millennium of consummation and peace. (*Improvement Era*, Apr. 1920, 514–515.)

Melvin J. Ballard

Melvin J. Ballard (1873–1939) was called to be an apostle in 1919, fulfilling a prophesy made by the Spirit while his mother still carried him in her womb. He was a grandfather of current apostle M. Russell Ballard.

Kindly turn your thoughts backward, if possible, beyond the period of your mortal existence, and look into the distant past by aid of memory and imagination, and think of those scenes that were enacted one hundred years ago when there was no state of Utah, no Salt Lake City, no Tabernacle; when the western bounds of civilization were far east of us; when, indeed, there were but nine million four hundred thousand persons in the United States.

That we may get a proper setting for the theme that is now to be presented, imagine a condition of religious enthusiasm spreading over the country so that it affected all the towns and hamlets of the land; men and women were leaving their occupations and camping by meetinghouses while daily and nightly revivals were being conducted. The debate and contentions between religious denominations were most intense, and often bitter. . . .

The echoes of these things reached the western part of the state of New York and affected the little community of Manchester, where the family of Joseph Smith resided. As a member of that household, though but a child, he, like other neighbors, had gathered in the assembly to be religiously instructed. The child, in that little gathering, had watched the performance, while various mourners went to confession and were immediately surrounded by eager ministers anxious to win the new convert to his particular persuasion. Various members of the family had responded and affiliated with one of the groups of worshipers. By the process of elimination, it reached the lad who had serious thoughts concerning his present predicament, and when he thought of his responding to the appeal, then the next problem that beset his mind was: "To which group shall I go?"

In the midst of these uncertainties, he read those inspired words in the epistle of James [1:5]. . . . He writes that never did scripture have such an effect upon the heart of man as these words of promise had upon his heart, and they moved him to action. Seeking a place where he might commune with God, he selected the little grove of standing timber, remaining as nature had planted it on a small portion of his father's farm. Within the seclusion of this grove he offered his humble petition to his Father. He informs us of the power of darkness that arrayed itself to destroy him. . . . But the Power that delivered him—the Power of Light—coming forth from the presence of our Father, triumphed, as it always shall triumph ultimately, over the powers of darkness.

In the midst of this glorious Presence the boy was comforted, reassured by those words spoken by the most glorious Being who exists in all the eternal worlds—our Father in heaven,—who said to the trembling youth, "Joseph"—and I fancy that the words, not only spoken as a Father would speak them, but in tenderness and in sympathy, removed all fear and doubt—"Joseph, this is my Beloved Son," and then introduced our Redeemer.

You know the answer that was given. That nowhere in the world was the truth to be found; the day of darkness was not only proclaimed, but the ending of that day of darkness was indicated in the assurance given by the visit of the Redeemer. The most wonderful, the most complete revelation of the powers that exist in heaven above and in the realms of the condemned, was here revealed. On this occasion, not only God's voice was heard, but his Being was revealed as well as the Being and the voice of his Son. . . . I knew as I know this night,—in the very depth of my heart and soul, and if every fiber of my being had a tongue, and every hair of my head could speak, it could testify as I do, that Joseph told the truth. God did manifest himself, the Redeemer did come, and all that I have—all that is worth while to me,—has come because Joseph told the truth.

. . . And in the dim future, so far away that we cannot now even think of what shall be, the memory of this visitation like the memory of the birth of Christ, shall remain as long as we live; and we shall live forever. (*Improvement Era,* June 1920, 693.)

John A. Widtsoe

John A. Widtsoe (1872–1952) was born in Norway and immigrated to Utah in 1883. He became a professor of agriculture at BYU, president of Utah State Agricultural College and the University of Utah, and Commissioner of Church Education. A prolific author of Church doctrinal works, he was called to be an apostle in 1921.

The formal story of the Church of Jesus Christ of Latter-day Saints begins with the First Vision of Joseph Smith. The Vision was the initial event in the restoration in the latter days of the Gospel of Jesus Christ. The message of the Vision is the most fundamental in the history of the Church, and explains clearly and tersely the need of a restoration. Moreover, the Vision was the beginning of a process of spiritual education under direct divine supervision of a boy who was destined in God's hands to be the instrument through which the restoration was accomplished.

The peculiarly fundamental nature of the Vision, both for the cause and the individual, gives assurance that the Vision embodies, well as any one event may do so, the spirit and genius of the whole work accomplished through the Prophet Joseph Smith. . . . The lessons of the First Vision are those that have guided thousands of honest hearts into the Church and that are directing today the lives of the sincere members of the Church.

The Reality of the Vision.—There are internal and external evidences of the simple and complete truthfulness of the First Vision which have satisfied thousands of serious investigators. For the purpose of this essay it is probably sufficient to say that God has before revealed himself to man in person, if sacred writ be believed, and what He has done He may do again.

The essential question that the reader of the First Vision must ask himself is "Does a God live?" If there be a God, He can certainly show himself and speak to his children. The pastime of limiting God might be condoned in a darker age when gods were man-made, but the God of truth which men of today know or seek is not subject to man's will or definitions. . . .

Men Are God's Instruments.—The youth of the Prophet Joseph Smith at the time of the First Vision and his humble extraction have often been commented upon in wonder. Yet, for youth to be commissioned to do great work is not unique in ecclesiastical history. Samuel heard the voice of God and carried out a heavy task at a very tender age and David was but a shepherd lad when he was anointed to become King of Israel. Both of these great men came from the people and not from the aristocracy. . . .

The fact that God initiated a vast, latter-day work by communicating with a boy barely into his teens, teaches the essential relationship between man and God. . . .

The First Vision teaches forcefully that men are God's instruments, and that God in choosing His instruments is no respecter of persons according to the standards of men. The all important concern of the individual is to be ready for service when the voice of the Almighty calls.

The Key to Heavenly Vision.—Joseph's desire to know the truth for himself was the key that unlocked the door to heavenly visions. . . .

This noble spirit of truth seeking, which in all ages has brought light out of darkness, made the First Vision possible, and made truth the foundation of the whole work. In fact, it is not conceivable that God would impose from without a knowledge of Himself upon a person who indifferently cared not for the security of his knowledge. . . .

To win the truth for one's self was the first step in the First Vision, and in the establishment of the Church. It is always the first step in the getting of sound knowledge by the individual. The chief characteristic of the followers of Joseph Smith is the desire to know truth for themselves. . . .

The truth loving boy did that which every honest truth-seeker does: he asked for knowledge. To refuse to accept a statement because it is not accompanied by proof and to stop there is paralyzing to intellect and conscience. Progress in truth comes when the seeker proceeds to ask for light and information. Every great work begins with a prayer. . . .

Josephs' prayer was heard. Just as certainly is every prayer of man heard, provided it is uttered in full faith in God, in his goodness and power. . . .

Joseph's prayer was answered. . . . It is possibly one of the most comforting lessons of the First Vision, that God, hears and answers prayer.

The Struggle from Within.—Hardly had the boy found a quiet grove, and uttered his prayer, when he was set upon by the power of evil. According to his own description the ordeal must have been fearfully trying. Before the battle was over the boy felt that his very life was in danger. . . .

First, there comes fear from within. Joseph, who had read the inspired message of James, was taking the Lord at his word. It seemed almost a preposterous thing to do. Would God answer? How would the answer come? Would he recognize the message if one came?

No wonder darkness and fear seized upon the boy. Every person who has set out in search of truth has had his prejudices, preconceived notions, doubts of success, and all sorts of apparently logical antagonisms rise up against him and his venture. Men all too often fail to realize the vast opposition to the acceptance of new truth that is heaped up within their own minds. Once the inward antagonisms have been overcome, progress may be expected.

It is not easy to be open minded. Let all remember that the evil within ourselves is always to be reckoned with and to be feared. Undoubtedly God chose deliberately the white soul of a boy upon which to write the latter-day message. . . .

The Opposition from Without.— . . . Joseph's love of truth, determination to find truth and willingness to travel the appointed way to truth was a challenge to evil. . . . Joseph emphasizes that this terrific struggle was not of an imaginary character, but was with the "power of some actual being from the unseen world." The Prophet further pays tribute to the might of this power when he says that this being "had such marvelous power as I had never before felt in any being." The boy was almost ready to give up his quest and "abandon himself to destruction."

The praying boy won. In the end, light will triumph over darkness, good over evil, truth will always be revealed if the seeker fail not in his search. It requires courage and effort and persistence, but the conquest is sure. Joseph exerted all his powers to call upon God for help. . . . There was fine pedagogic propose in Joseph's battle with *evil*, as it gave him a contrast with the glory he was about to experience.

Light, the Sign of Truth.—When the youthful prophet had fought off the evil powers from within and without, the vision began. An effulgent light gradually filled the grove, until, according to Orson Pratt who dwelt in the Prophet's household and no doubt had often heard the Prophet relate the story, every leaf, twig, and branch stood out distinct against the bright light. . . .

Abundant light filled the grove, and the soul of the boy was again at peace, when two personages, "whose beauty and glory defy all description" descended as it were out of the sky. When these personages rested before the boy, one of them called Joseph by name, pointed to the other and said: "This is my beloved Son, hear Him." This was the first direct message of God to the boy who was to become God's instrument in the restoration of the Church of Christ.

The full import of these words is such as to justify their use as the fundamental message to man.

God, the Father, the supreme ruler of the universe, was present, yet he recognized the place of His Son, to whom had been assigned the care of affairs pertaining to this earth, and requested that He be heard. It was an eloquent lesson in respect for law and order. . . .

Personality of Godhood.—Before the boy stood two personages, God the Father and God the Son. It was their first recorded appearance for many centuries. During the lapse of time, controversy had raged concerning the form and nature of God. The current belief made God a personage of spirit of most extraordinary properties. So small was he said to be as to be able to dwell in a man's heart, and so vast as to fill the whole universe. The Father, Son, and Holy Ghost were literally three in one. God had become an intangible, incomprehensible being, and man was forced away from a God whom he could not understand.

In the First Vision was a revelation of God and of Godhood. The two Gods before the boy were like unto men though of a surpassing and indescribable glory. They spoke with voices like unto men. They were distinct and separate personalities. God could be seen; could speak; could be heard; could be understood! It became clear that men are of the race of Gods, and the very children of God. It must then be that God is Master because of a superior power based on superior knowledge and wisdom. The confusion concerning the nature of God was blown away at a breath. The knowledge of God, which men had originally received but confounded with fanciful imagination, was in a moment restored. . . .

The work of Joseph Smith rests wholly upon the conviction that God lives, and is a personal being, of transcendent attributes, but who may in part at least be understood by man.

Untruth Is an Abomination.—Joseph Smith had gone into the Grove to learn, if he could, which of all the contending sects in his neighborhood was the right one and which one he should join, and this question he put to the heavenly personages which stood before him.

The answer was an astounding one. He was answered that he "must join none of them, for they were all wrong; all their creeds were an abomination in (God's) sight; that those professors were all corrupt."

Probably nothing could have surprised the boy more than this answer. Surely no part of the message delivered to the world by Joseph Smith has given more offense to many honest souls who in all sincerity and with noble lives have conformed to the practices of their churchly faith—faiths which gradually, through the centuries had strayed from the full truth.

Yet Joseph had come to inquire for truth, the whole, untarnished, unmixed truth. God deals only in truth, and cannot palliate untruth. . . . No matter how sincerely untruth is believed in, it is still untruth and perhaps more dangerous because it is not recognized as untruth. Harsh as the message may have seemed to the boy and to many who have read the First Vision, yet no one, who is of sincere heart, could wish that Divinity should sugar coat the bitterness or whiten the blackness of error. . . .

The Need of Doctrinal Completeness.—However, the divine denunciation was of creeds or religious systems. A creed is made up of many doctrines for the guidance of man. Nearly all modern religions accept, for the guidance of man, the ten commandments and the fundamental principles of Christian ethics; and contain no doubt some truth and much good. . . .

As creeds the churches appealing to the boy were wrong, but there was no wholesale denunciation of every belief or practice included within the creeds. . . .

The boy was told not to join any of the sects, contending for membership, yet was not given a full outline of the plan of salvation. It was more than three years later that he had his next vision, and even then the requisite knowledge came to him little by little. . . .

From out the First Vision grew a marvelous work and a wonder—a church of vitality, ever growing as new visions have come and do come to its leaders and to its members. . . .

The Physical Cost of Truth.—When the heavenly beings had departed, and the boy came to himself, he found himself lying on his back, looking into heaven, but with his physical strength largely spent. It was only after recovering his strength in some degree that he was able to go home, and even then, as he was leaning against the fireplace, his mother noticed his exhaustion and made comment on it.

It was Joseph's first realization of the fierce cost of truth. Knowledge does not come unsought, or without effort on the part of the learner. It required effort to go into the grove to pray. It required terrific effort to fight away the evil powers that sought to keep knowledge from him. It required an intense application of body and spirit to keep in tune with Divinity so that the heavenly message might indeed be his. Naturally the boy was exhausted. But, who would not gladly pay the price for such a vision! . . .

The Results of the Vision.—The vision was over. The boy who had communed with God stood in the humble home by the fireplace. The mother was moving about with her homely duties. How did the boy feel concerning his experiment in discovering truth for himself?

In answer to his mother's anxious question concerning his welfare he answered, "All is well," and added, "I have learned for myself that Presbyterianism is not true."

It was the word of the triumphant conqueror. A few hours before, Joseph had set out to learn the truth for himself and now he declared that he knew the truth "for himself." His triumph was such that there was neither place nor feeling for many words.

That he mentioned Presbyterianism rather than any of the other "isms" that sought converts was of course simply because his mother and several of his family had affiliated themselves with the Presbyterian communion. He knew that all the sects were wrong. . . .

The Later Work.—The boy Joseph Smith had seen God and conversed with Him. Joseph's prayer had been answered. Doubt no longer lingered within his mind.

To his family he told the marvelous story of the Vision; it was listened to gravely and with respect. All the members of his family in time became convinced of the truthfulness of this vision and the later ones and became his followers and defenders of the message he was called to restate to the world.

Some few days after the Vision he told his story also to one of the preachers who were leading the religious excitement in the neighborhood. To his surprise it was scoffed at. He was told that visions had ceased, and that God no longer spoke from the heavens. Worse than that, the telling of the story awakened a prejudice which grew into a persistent persecution which lasted throughout his life. . . .

Meanwhile, the boy, after three years of the ordinary life of humbly placed lads of the time and place, had other visions in which the fundamental truths of the First Vision were amplified and extended. In course of time he became the inspired translator of a holy record of ancient America, and later the organizer under God of the Church of Jesus Christ of Latter-day Saints—the old church restored in latter days. All his days were devoted, in poverty and under bitter persecution, to the service of the Church, and he became at last a martyr in its cause. (*Young Woman's Journal*, Apr. 1920, 179–191.)

Heavenly beings . . . appeared and spoke to the boy [Joseph]. The one said, pointing to the other, "This is my beloved Son; hear Him." Then the Son spoke and gave the information that the boy wanted. Herein lies two great lessons which run through all of Mormonism.

First, divinity is personal. . . . We in this day can hardly understand the greatness of that message, for in that day men were taught that God could not or would not speak anymore. . . . This is the first and greatest testimony of the Prophet. God is a personal being who speaks, who can express his feelings and emotions. Joseph could talk to him as he would to his earthly father. Joseph Smith asked his question. Then the answer came. . . .

The second lesson from the appearance of the heavenly beings is that the Father did not engage in conversation with the boy, beyond saying, "This is my beloved Son; hear Him." That also reads an eternal lesson which should be heeded among all men. It was a simple lesson: order must prevail among us. Jesus was called to create this world, under the direction of the Father, which he did in preparation for our coming. Later he came in person to atone for our sins.

The Father recognized his commission as the creator and redeemer of the world; therefore, called upon the Son to answer Joseph's question. The law of order rules the universe. (Speech, Logan Utah Institute, 1946, 3–4.)

Joseph F. Merrill

Joseph F. Merrill (1868–1952), son of apostle Marriner W. Merrill, was the first native Utahn to receive a PhD. He taught physics and chemistry at the University of Utah, became Commissioner of Church Education, and created the church's institutes of religion. He was called to be and apostle in 1931.

Aside from Jesus Christ, I [look] upon [Joseph Smith] as second in greatness to no other religious teacher that ever lived. And judged by the same standard used in judging greatness in men—by his works—as with Shakespeare, Washington, Lincoln, Einstein, etc.—I still believe my view of him is correct and that he is the greatest man America ever produced. Hence I am convinced that he is deserving of a careful, thorough, and honest study by every person interested in his personal well-being. According to first-class evidence, Joseph Smith did actually, really see and hear the Father and the Son, two highly glorified beings, . . . in whose image man himself is made. (Conference Report, Apr. 1948, 70.)

J. Reuben Clark Jr.

J. Reuben Clark Jr. (1871–1961) was an attorney who became an Undersecretary of State under U.S. President Calvin Coolidge and the U.S. Ambassador to Mexico. He was called to be an apostle in 1934 and served as a counselor to three Church presidents.

There are for the Church and for each and all of its members, two prime things which may not be overlooked, forgotten, shaded, or discarded:

First: That Jesus Christ is the Son of God, the Only Begotten of the Father in the flesh, the Creator of the world, the Lamb of God, the Sacrifice for the sins of the world, the Atoner for Adam's transgression. . . .

The second of the two things to which we must all give full faith is that the Father and the Son actually and in truth and very deed appeared to the Prophet Joseph in a vision in the woods; that other heavenly visions followed to Joseph and to others; that the gospel and the Holy Priesthood after the Order of the Son of God were in truth and fact restored to the earth from which they were lost by the apostasy of the primitive Church. . . .

Without these two great beliefs the Church would cease to be the Church. (Speech, BYU Summer School, Aspen Grove, UT, 8 Aug. 1938, 3, 7.)

Marion G. Romney

Marion G. Romney (1897–1988) was an attorney who was called as one of the first Assistants to the Twelve. After serving in that position for ten years, he was called as an apostle. He served as a counselor to two Church presidents.

Some people have said that Joseph Smith was an unlearned man. He was an unlearned man in the things of the world, but the day he came out of the grove, following the first vision, he was the most learned person in the world in the things that count. When he came out of that grove, he knew more than all the world put together about the great question of the resurrection, which had been argued from the time man began to think seriously, because he had seen standing before him, the resurrected Christ. When he came out of that grove, he knew more about the nature of God than all the world.

There had been many books written; philosophers had spent their lives trying to find out the nature of God, but when God took Joseph in hand to reach him, he cut through all material things and taught Joseph the truth about these and many other important things. (Conference Report, Apr. 1946, 37.)

Hugh B. Brown

Hugh B. Brown (1883–1975) was an attorney from Canada who served as an Assistant to the Twelve for five years. He was called as an apostle in 1958 and served as a counselor to David O. McKay.

When Joseph came out of the woods, he had at least four fundamental truths, and he announced them to the world. First, that the Father and the Son are separate and distinct individuals. Secondly, that the canon of scripture is not complete. Thirdly, that man was created in the bodily image of God. And fourth, the channel between earth and heaven is open and revelation is continuous. (*BYU Speeches,* 4 Oct. 1955, 8.)

N. Eldon Tanner

N. Eldon Tanner (1898–1982) was a politician in Canada who served as an Assistant to the Twelve for two years. He was called as apostle in 1962, and he served as a counselor in the First Presidency to four Church presidents.

The one prayer which impressed me was when Joseph Smith went into the woods to pray. He had read, "If any of you lack wisdom, let him ask of God, that giveth to all men liberally, . . . and it shall be given." If *any of you* lack wisdom, ask of God and you will receive your answer. Pray with faith, not wavering. "For he that wavereth is like a wave of the sea driven with the wind and tossed." (James 1:6.)

God the Father and his Son, Jesus Christ, appeared to Joseph—actually appeared to him—and told him they had a work for him to do. He had talked to God; God heard his prayers; his prayers were answered. (*Ensign,* May 1981, 50.)

Bruce R. McConkie

Bruce R. McConkie (1915–1985) was called to serve in the First Council of the Seventy in 1946 and an apostle in 1972. A prolific author of doctrinal works, Elder McConkie was the son-in-law of church apostle and president Joseph Fielding Smith.

The First Vision . . . is rated as first both from the standpoint of time and of pre-eminent importance. In it Joseph Smith saw and conversed with the Father and the Son, both of which exalted personages were personally present before him as he lay enwrapped in the Spirit and overshadowed by the Holy Ghost.

This transcendent vision was the beginning of latter day revelation; it marked the opening of the heavens after the long night of apostate darkness. . . . This vision was the most important event that had taken place in all world history from the day of Christ's ministry to the glorious hour when it occurred. . . .

If this inexperienced youth had been seeking to fabricate some great spiritual experience, he never in the world would have come back with a story that struck irreconcilably at all the creeds of Christendom and all the teachings he himself had so far received. . . . In an attempt to deceive he might have said that an angel appeared, or that some other miraculous event transpired, but never would it have occurred to him to rock the whole religious foundation of the Christian world with such a startling claim as that which he did make. . . .

Evidences of the reality of the First Vision might be multiplied, but the greatest proofs that it took place are the whisperings of the Spirit to the devout truth seekers and the establishment and triumph of The Church of Jesus Christ of Latter-day Saints. (McConkie, *Mormon Doctrine* [1966], 204–206.)

We are all acquainted with the First Vision in which the Prophet saw the Father and the Son standing above him in a pillar of light—holy beings, personages who defied description because of the glory and grandeur that attended them (JS–H 2:16–17). We are aware that they are personal beings (D&C 130:22–23). This First Vision is the beginning of the knowledge of God in this dispensation. In just a few moments of the opening of the heavens, the Lord swept away all the false concepts, the Apostasy, the cobwebs of the past, and once again there was one man on earth who knew that God was a personal being in whose image man is created. . . .

That is the beginning of the revelation of the knowledge of God in our day. (BYU Devotional, 4 Jan. 1972.)

David B. Haight

David B. Haight (1906–2004) was the mayor of Palo Alto, California who served as an Assistant to the Twelve for six years. He was called to be an apostle in 1976. When he died at age ninety-seven, he was the oldest man to have served as a member of the Quorum of the Twelve Apostles in this dispensation.

Since my early youth I have believed and carried in my mind a vivid picture of the teenage Joseph finding a secluded spot, kneeling in the quiet grove, and in childlike faith asking the desire of his heart. He must have felt assured the Lord would hear and somehow answer him. There appeared to him two glorious personages, a description of whom, he said, was beyond his ability to express. . . .

The events related by Joseph Smith of the Restoration are true.

Each of you can develop in your bosom an uplifting, sanctifying, and glorifying feeling of its truth. The Holy Ghost will reveal and seal upon each of your hearts this knowledge, if you truly desire. Our understanding, belief, and faith in "the vision" (as we refer to it) of God the Father and his Only Begotten Son appearing to Joseph, thereby ushering in this final dispensation with its great and precious truths, is essential to our eternal salvation. . . .

The knowledge is mine that God did reveal himself unto Joseph—his witness of this final dispensation. We now know something of the form, features, and even character of that mighty intelligence whose wisdom, creation, and power control the affairs of the universe.

God made it known that Jesus Christ is the express image of the Father. (BYU Devotional, 2 Mar. 1986, 2.)

James E. Faust

James E. Faust (1920–2007) was an attorney and politician in Utah who served as an Assistant to the Twelve and member of First Quorum of the Seventy for six years. He was called to be an apostle in 1978 and later served as a counselor in the First Presidency.

There has been no event more glorious, more controversial, nor more important in the story of Joseph Smith than this vision. It is possibly the most singular event to occur on the earth since the Resurrection. . . .

What was learned from the First Vision?

1. The existence of God our Father as a personal being, and proof that man was made in the image of God.

2. That Jesus is a personage, separated and distinct from the Father.

3. That Jesus Christ is declared by the Father to be his Son.

4. That Jesus was the conveyer of revelation as taught in the Bible.

5. The promise of James to ask of God for wisdom was fulfilled.

6. The reality of an actual being from an unseen world who tried to destroy Joseph Smith.

7. That there was a falling away from the Church established by Jesus Christ—Joseph was told not to join any of the sects, for they taught the doctrines of men.

8. Joseph Smith became a witness for God and his Son, Jesus Christ. (*Ensign,* May 1984, 67–68.)

Neal A. Maxwell

Neal A. Maxwell (1926–2004) was an educator and prolific author of Church doctrinal works who served as an Assistant to the Twelve and a member of First Quorum of the Seventy for seven years. He was called to be an apostle in 1981.

Joseph was a good man, but he was called by a perfect Lord, Jesus of Nazareth! He received his first counsel from God the Father: "This is My Beloved Son. Hear Him!" (JS–H 1:17.) Joseph listened carefully to Jesus then and ever after. . . . Joseph Smith was . . . an eyewitness of the resurrected Christ. (*Ensign*, Aug. 1986, 11.)

M. Russell Ballard

M. Russell Ballard (1928–present) served in the First Quorum of the Seventy for nine years and was called to be an apostle in 1985. A grandson of apostles Melvin J. Ballard and Hyrum M. Smith, Elder Ballard is a direct descendant of Hyrum Smith, brother of Joseph.

In the spring of 1820, a pillar of light illuminated a grove of trees in upstate New York. Our Heavenly Father and His Beloved Son appeared to the Prophet Joseph Smith. This experience began the restoration of powerful doctrinal truths that had been lost for centuries. Among those truths that had been dimmed by the darkness of apostasy was the stirring reality that we are all the spirit sons and daughters of a loving God who is our Father. We are part of His family. He is not a father in some allegorical or poetic sense. He is literally the Father of our spirits. He cares for each one of us. . . . In that unprecedented appearance of the Father and the Son in the Sacred Grove, the very first word spoken by the Father of us all was the personal name of Joseph. Such is our Father's personal relationship with each of us. He knows our names and yearns for us to become worthy to return to live with Him. (*Ensign,* May 2004, 84.)

Jeffrey R. Holland

Jeffrey R. Holland (1940–present) served as president of BYU and as Commissioner of Church Education. He was a member of the First Quorum of the Seventy for five years and was called to be an apostle in 1994.

Joseph Smith's 19th-century frontier environment was aflame with competing crowds of Christian witnesses. But in the tumult they created, these exuberant revivalists were, ironically, obscuring the very Savior young Joseph so earnestly sought. Battling what he called "darkness and confusion," he retreated to the solitude of a grove of trees where he saw and heard a more glorious witness of the Savior's centrality to the gospel than anything we have mentioned here this morning [in conference]. With a gift of sight unimagined and unanticipated, Joseph beheld in vision his Heavenly Father, the great God of the universe, and Jesus Christ, His perfect Only Begotten Son. Then the Father set the example . . . : He pointed to Jesus, saying: "This is My Beloved Son. Hear Him!" No greater expression of Jesus's divine identity, His primacy in the plan of salvation, and His standing in the eyes of God could ever exceed that short seven-word declaration. (*Ensign,* Nov. 2019, 7–8.)

Henry B. Eyring

Henry B. Eyring (1933–present) was a professor of business at Stanford University, Commissioner of Church Education, and president of Ricks College. He later served ten years in the Presiding Bishopric and First Quorum of the Seventy and was called as an apostle in 1995. He has been a counselor to three presidents of the Church.

Trust comes from knowing God. . . . My heart is filled with gratitude for what God has revealed about Himself that we might trust Him.

For me it began in 1820 with a young boy in a grove of trees on a farm in the state of New York. The boy, Joseph Smith Jr., walked among the trees to a secluded spot. He knelt to pray with complete trust that God would answer his pleading to know what he should do to be cleansed and saved through the Atonement of Jesus Christ.

Each time I read his account, my trust in God and His servants expands. . . . The Father revealed to us that He lives, that Jesus Christ is His Beloved Son, and that He loved us enough to send that Son to save us, who are His children. (*Ensign*, Nov. 2010, 72.)

Dieter F. Uchtdorf

Dieter F. Uchtdorf (1940–present) was born in an area that is now part of Czech Republic. He became a commercial pilot and was a member of the Quorums of the Seventy for ten years. He was called to be an apostle in 2004 and has served as a counselor to two Church presidents.

This is how Joseph Smith's First Vision blesses our own personal lives, the lives of families, and eventually the whole human family—we come to believe in Jesus Christ through the testimony of the Prophet Joseph Smith. . . .

God has spoken to Joseph Smith for the purpose of blessing all of God's children with His mercy and love, even in times of uncertainties and insecurities, of wars and rumors of wars, of natural and personal disasters. . . .

Through our faith in the personal witness of the Prophet Joseph and the reality of the First Vision, through study and prayer, deep and sincere, we will be blessed with a firm faith in the Savior of the world, who spoke to Joseph "on the morning of a beautiful, clear day, early in the spring of eighteen hundred and twenty" (Joseph Smith—History 1:14). (*Ensign*, Feb. 2009, 7.)

Part 4

ADDITIONAL TEACHINGS AND TESTIMONIES

ABOUT THE FIRST VISION

Powerful testimonies of the reality of Joseph Smith's First Vision are not the sole province of prophets and apostles. For two centuries, thousands and millions of everyday people have developed their own conviction that God the Father and Jesus Christ, His Son, did indeed appear to young Joseph Smith in a grove of trees in 1820. These have included farmers and carpenters and bricklayers, teachers and nurses and engineers, physicists and auto mechanics and soldiers, merchants and factory workers and doctors, miners and waitresses and accountants. People from all walks of life, from nearly every nation, from all races, from all religions and creeds, both young and old, rich and poor, and male and female have received, through the Holy Ghost, a testimony that Joseph Smith was a prophet of God and that the remarkable story he told of visions and plates and angelic ordinations was literally and factually true.

Even those prophets and apostles quoted earlier did not receive their testimonies through a special dispensation that came because of their Church positions. Instead, they received personal witnesses of Jesus Christ and of his prophet, Joseph Smith, far earlier, when they would have been considered "everyday people." Then, because they continued valiant in what they had received, and because the Lord had need of their talents and abilities in guiding His Church, they were placed in positions of influence, where they could share those testimonies with many others.

In 1920 The Church of Jesus Christ of Latter-day Saints celebrated the one hundredth anniversary of the First Vision. The entire April 1920 issue of the Church's official magazine for adults, the *Improvement Era,* was devoted to articles, poetry, and printed music about the First Vision. Each member of the First Presidency at the time—Heber J. Grant, Anthon H. Lund, and Charles W. Penrose—contributed an article. Apostles David O. McKay, Joseph Fielding Smith, James E. Talmage, and John A. Widtsoe each shared teachings and testimonies, addressing not only the First Vision but also the flood of light and blessings that had poured out on the earth as a result of the vision and its aftermath. Orson F. Whitney of the Quorum of the Twelve published part of an epic poem about the gospel of Jesus Christ and its restoration through Joseph Smith.

Andrew Jenson, long-time assistant Church historian, described how, after the heavens were opened to the young Joseph Smith, the gospel had been sent forth to all nations. He concluded by commenting on Jehovah's declaration to Joseph that His church was not to be found anywhere on earth: "After our elders have visited nearly every land and clime in the whole world and have investigated the religious conditions among Christians, Jews, Mohammedans, and Pagans, they [the elders] have become absolutely convinced that the statements made by the boy prophet Joseph Smith in western New York, early in the spring of 1820, are true. The boy prophet could not possibly have known the condition of the world as he explained it; but the great Master, the founder of Christianity, knew, and he told the praying boy the facts which one hundred years of careful investigation and experience have proved to be true." (*Improvement Era,* Apr. 1920, 553.)

Finally, beginning in the April 1920 *Improvement Era,* the Church published a series of seven lessons on the Prophet Joseph Smith, designed to be taught in all Mutual Improvement Association meetings in the Church during April, May, and June of that year. (*Improvement Era,* Apr. 1920, 560–575.)

Many of the offerings in that *Improvement Era,* and of the April general conference that year, are found in the pages of this book (both in sections 3 and 4). Of course, many leaders, teachers, scholars, missionaries, and parents have continued to teach and testify of the divine calling of Joseph Smith, beginning with his supernal vision in the Sacred Grove and continuing throughout his entire life.

This section of the book brings together testimonies and teachings of individuals who were not prophets and apostles. It includes General Authority Seventies, historians, and writers. Some, such as B. H. Roberts, Truman Madsen, and Richard Bushman, are familiar to many Church members. Others, although knowledgeable and talented, are not as well known, including Susa Young Gates, Charles H. Hart, and Nephi Jensen. These statements are arranged in chronological order. Where more than one statement from an individual is used, the quotations are organized together, with the earliest statement presented first.

B. H. Roberts

B. H. Roberts (1857–1933) served in the First Council of the Seventy from 1888 to his death. He also was Assistant Church Historian for the last thirty years of his life, during which he wrote and published thousands of pages of Church history and doctrine.

Religious Agitations.—While the Smith family lived in Manchester, when Joseph was in his fifteenth year, there was an unusual excitement on the subject of religion. It began with the Methodists, but soon became general among all the sects, and union revival meetings, in which all sects, took part were held in the vicinity of Manchester. The Smith family, being by nature religiously inclined became interested in these meetings, and several of them, viz., Joseph's mother, his brothers Hyrum and

Samuel Harrison, and his sisters Lucy and Sophronia, were converted to the Presbyterian faith. Joseph's own mind was much wrought up by this religious agitation. . . .

In the midst of the war of words and tumult of opinion that accompanied this agitation, Joseph would often say to himself, What is to be done? Who of all these parties are right?

Joseph Smith's First Prayer and Vision.—While floundering in the midst of these difficulties he came to the following passage in the first chapter of the Epistle of James:

"If any of you lack wisdom, let him ask of God, that giveth to all men liberally, and upbraideth not; and it shall be given him."

This passage impressed him with great force. It was the voice of God to him. If any man lacked wisdom he did; and here was counsel given directly how to obtain it, with a promise that he should receive it and not be unbraided for asking. He at last decided to follow the divine injunction.

It was in the morning of a beautiful, clear day, early in the spring of eighteen hundred and twenty, that Joseph put his resolution into effect. He selected a place in a grove near his father's house for that purpose. It was his first attempt to pray vocally, and he was somewhat timid; but finding himself alone he knelt down and began to offer up the desires of his heart to the Lord. He had scarcely began to pray when he was seized by some power which threw him violently to the ground, and it seemed for a time that he was doomed to a sudden destruction. It was no imaginary power but some actual being from the unseen world. His tongue for a time was bound that he could not speak; darkness gathered about him; but exerting all his powers he called upon God to deliver him out of the hands of his enemy, and at the very moment he was ready to give up in despair and abandon himself to destruction, he beheld a pillar of light immediately over his head descending towards him. Its brightness was above that of the sun at noon-day, and no sooner did it appear than he was freed from the enemy which had held him bound.

When the light rested upon him he beheld within it two personages standing above him in the air, whose brightness and glory defy all description, but they exactly resembled each other in form and features. One of them, pointing to the other said: "JOSEPH, THIS IS MY BELOVED SON, HEAR HIM."

Joseph's purpose in calling upon the Lord was to learn which of the sects was right, that he might know which to join. As soon, therefore, as he gained his self-possession, he addressed these questions to the personage to whom he was directed. To his astonishment he was told that none of the sects were right, and that he must join none of them. He was further told by the person who addressed him, that all their creeds were an abomination in his sight; that those professors were all corrupt; that they drew near to him with their lips, but their hearts were far from him; that they taught for doctrine the commandments of men; that they had a form of godliness, but denied the power of God. And he was commanded the second time to join none of them.

There were many other things which Jesus said to Joseph on this occasion, but the prophet never recorded them further than to say that he received a promise that the fullness of the gospel would at some future time be made known to him.

The Importance of the Vision.—This splendid revelation is of vast importance: First, it dispels the vagaries that men had conjured up in respect to the person of Deity. Instead of being a personage without body, parts or passions, it revealed the fact that he had both body and parts, that he was in the form of man, or rather, that man had been made in his image.* Second: It clearly proves that the Father and Son are distinct persons, and not one person as the Christian world believes. The oneness of the Godhead, so frequently spoken of in scripture, must therefore relate to oneness of sentiment and agreement in purpose. Third: It swept away the rubbish of human dogma and tradition that had accumulated in all the ages since Messiah's personal ministry on earth, by announcing that God did not acknowledge any of the sects of Christendom as his church, nor their creeds as his gospel. Thus the ground was cleared for the planting of the truth. Fourth: it showed how mistaken the Christian world was in claiming that all revelation had ceased—that God would no more reveal himself to man. Fifth: the vision created a witness for God on the earth: a man lived who could say to some purpose that God lived and that Jesus was the Christ, for he had seen and talked with them. Thus was laid the foundation for faith. (Roberts, *Outlines of Ecclesiastical History* [1893], 276–279.)

[A] wave of religious fervor . . . passed over the western part of the State of New York in the winter and spring of 1820. The movement at that time was of unusual interest, first on account of its extent, and second on account of the intensity of the religious excitement produced. It can well be imagined that with these two conditions existing, the bitterness among the sects taking part in the movement would be correspondingly great when it came to dividing up the spoils. By which I mean when the converts made by a unity of effort began to file off some to one sect and some to another. Such was the case. Presbyterians opposed Methodists, and Methodists Baptists; and Baptists opposed both the other sects. All was strife, contention, confusion, beneath which Christian charity and good will to man—these weightier matters of the law—were buried so far out of sight that it might be questioned if they ever existed.

Standing somewhat apart from, but watching with intense interest this religious excitement, and wondering greatly at the confusion and strife attendant upon it was a lad fourteen years old. He was born of parents numbered among the pioneers of the wilderness, and up to that time had lived with them surrounded by the conditions already described in the [present book] as so favorable to morality and the development of religious sentiment. By this religious agitation the mind of the lad was stirred to serious reflection accompanied with great uneasiness on account of the sectarian strife so incessant and so bitter. . . .

Young as he was, his native intelligence taught him that something was radically wrong with all this contention over religion. It was clear even to his boyish mind that God could not be the author of all this confusion. God's church would not be split up into factions in this fashion; if he taught one society to worship one way, and administer one set of ordinances, he would not teach another principles diametrically opposed.

Influenced by these reflections he refrained from joining any of the sects and in the meantime studied the scriptures as best he could for himself. While thus engaged he came to that passage in James which says: "If any of you lack wisdom, let him ask of God, that giveth to all men liberally and upbraideth not and it shall be given him." That passage was like the voice of God to his spirit. "Never," he was wont to say in later life — "never did any passage of scripture come with more power to the heart of man than this did at this time to mine. It seemed to enter with great force into every feeling of my heart." He reflected upon it again and again, and as he did so the impression grew stronger that the advice of the ancient apostle offered a solution to his perplexities. . . .

Through the innocent eyes of a mere boy, he looked the proposition of James squarely in the front, and, thanks to the teachings of parents who revered the word of God, he believed what the man of God said, and he believed further that he expressed that which the Lord inspired him to say; so that it came to him with the full force of a revelation. Under such circumstances what was more natural than for him to reason thus: If any person needs wisdom from God, I do. . . . And since he gives wisdom to them that lack wisdom, and will give liberally and not upbraid, he thought he might venture. And so at last he did. He selected a place in a grove near his father's house, and there one beautiful morning in the spring of 1820, after looking timidly about to ascertain that he was alone, the boy knelt in his first attempt at vocal prayer, to ask God for wisdom.

No sooner had he begun calling upon the Lord than there sprang upon him a being from the unseen world, who so entirely overcame him, and bound his utterance, that he could not speak. Thick darkness gathered about him, and it seemed to the struggling boy that he was doomed to sudden destruction. He still exerted all his power to call upon the Lord to deliver him from the power of the enemy who had seized him. But still his unseen though none the less real enemy continued to prevail. Despair filled his heart. He was about to abandon himself to destruction when at the moment of his greatest alarm he saw a pillar of light exactly over his head, above the brightness of the sun, which descended gradually until it fell upon him. No sooner did this light appear than he was free from the enemy which had held him bound. As the light rested upon him he saw within it two personages whose brightness and glory defy all description. They stood above him in the air, and one of them pointing to the other said: "JOSEPH, THIS IS MY BELOVED SON, HEAR HIM."

The object of the lad in going to that place to engage in secret prayer was to learn of God which of all the sects was right, that he might know which to join. No sooner, therefore, did he recover his self-possession than he asked the personage to whom he was thus introduced, which of all the sects was right—which he should join. He was answered that he must join none of them; for they were all wrong. . . .

Many other things were said to him on that occasion which the Prophet has not recorded, except to say that he was promised that the fullness of the gospel would at some future time be made known to him.

With this the vision closed, and the boy on coming to himself was lying upon his back looking up into heaven. He arose to his feet and looked upon the place of his fierce struggle with his unseen though powerful enemy—the place also of his splendid vision! . . .

Let us consider the wide-sweeping effect of this boy's vision upon the accepted theology of Christendom.

First, it was a flat contradiction to the assumption that revelation had ceased, that God had no further communication to make to man.

Second, it reveals the errors into which men had fallen concerning the personages of the Godhead. It makes it manifest that God is not an incorporeal being without body, or parts; on the contrary he appeared to the Prophet in the form of a man, as he did to the ancient prophets. Thus after centuries of controversy the simple truth of the scriptures which teach that man was created in the likeness of God—hence God must be the same in form as man—was reaffirmed.

Third, it corrected the error of the theologians respecting the oneness of the persons of the Father and the Son. Instead of being one in person as the theologians taught, they are distinct in their persons, as much so as any father and son on earth; and the oneness of the Godhead referred to in the scriptures, must have reference to unity of purpose and of will; the mind of the one being the mind of the other, and so as to the will and other attributes.

The announcement of these truths, coupled with that other truth proclaimed by the Son of God, viz.: that none of the sects and churches of Christendom were acknowledged as the church or kingdom of God, furnish the elements for a religious revolution that will affect the very foundations of modern Christian theology. In a moment all the rubbish concerning religion which had accumulated through all the centuries since the gospel and authority to administer its ordinances had been taken from the earth, was grandly swept aside—the living rocks of truth were made bare upon which the Church of Christ was to be founded—a New Dispensation of the gospel was about to be committed to the earth—God had raised up a witness for himself among the children of men. (Roberts, *A New Witness for God* [1895], 167–174.)

In nothing have men so far departed from revealed truth as in their conceptions of God. Therefore, when it pleased the Lord in these last days to open again direct communication with men, by a new dispensation of the gospel, it is not surprising that the very first revelation given was one that revealed himself and his Son Jesus Christ. A revelation which not only made known the *being* of God, but the *kind* of a being he is. The Prophet Joseph Smith, in his account of his first great revelation, declares that he saw "two personages," resembling each other in form and features, but whose brightness and glory defied all description. One of these personages addressed the prophet and said, as he pointed to the other—

"This is my beloved Son, hear him."

This was the revelation with which the work of God in the last days began. The revelation of God, the Father; and of God, the Son. They were seen to be two distinct personages. They were like men in form; but infinitely more glorious in appearance, because perfect and divine. The Old Testament truth was reaffirmed by this revelation—"God created man in his own image, in the image of God created he him." Also the truth of the New Testament was reaffirmed—Jesus Christ was shown to be the express image of the Father's person, hence God, the Father, was in form like the Man, Christ Jesus, who is also called "the Son of Man." (Roberts, *The Mormon Doctrine of Deity* [1903], 3–4.)

For some years previous to 1830 western New York and Pennsylvania, as well as the states of Ohio and Kentucky, were the scenes of a great religious agitation. It was during these years that the revival camp-meeting system of sectarian propaganda was inaugurated. Scenes of wildest religious fervor and excitement were common. According to one writer upon the subject, "the people were accustomed to assemble, sometimes to the number of ten or twelve thousand, and they often continued together, in devotional exercises, for several days and nights." (J. B. Turner, *Mormonism in All Ages,* 1842, p. 272.) This was said of what was called the great revival in Kentucky in 1800. Later, as this method of reaching men with "religion" became more popular, the crowds were even larger and the encampments extended through many weeks. "Such was the eagerness of the people to attend," says Henry Howe, author of "Historical Collections of the Great West," that entire neighborhoods were forsaken, and the roads literally crowded by those pressing forward on their way to the grove." (*Historical Collections of the Great West,* p. 205.) The great assemblies being too large for one person to address them, they would divide into several congregations and be addressed by as many different speakers. . . .

Palmyra, New York, the home of the Smiths, was in the zone of this widespread religious agitation. In the spring of 1820 the ministers of the several churches in and about Palmyra decided upon a "union revival," in order to "convert the unconverted." The Presbyterians, Methodists and Baptists were the sects represented, and the Reverend Mr. Stockton of the Presbyterian church was the leading spirit of the movement, and chairman of the meetings. It was during this revival that the Prophet's mother, her two sons, Hyrum and Samuel Harrison, and her daughter Sophronia became members of the Presbyterian church. Joseph Smith, Sen., was unmoved amid the universal excitement.

Joseph Smith, Jr., was much wrought up in his spirit, . . . and [the] divisions that existed between these several churches perplexed him. . . . Unaided reason taught him that unity must be a characteristic of the Church of Christ. . . .

After much reflection . . . , he at last took his resolution. He would put the doctrine of James to the test. He would ask God for wisdom. . . . Situated directly west of the Smith home, a few hundred yards distant, yet on their own farm, was a beautiful grove sufficiently dense and removed from the road to give the necessary seclusion the youth desired; and here on the morning of a beautiful, clear day in that early spring time, he knelt for the first time in all his life to make a personal, direct, verbal appeal to God in prayer.

And now something strange happened. The youth had just began timidly to express the desires of his heart in words, when he was seized upon by an invisible power that overcame him; his tongue was bound so that he could not speak. Darkness gathered about him, and it seemed for a time that he was doomed to sudden destruction. He exerted all his powers to call upon God for deliverance from this enemy—not from a merely "imaginary ruin," as he assures us, "but from the power of some actual being from the unseen world," who possessed such strength as the youth had never before encountered. Despair seized upon him, and he felt that he must abandon himself to destruction. At this moment of dreadful alarm he saw a pillar of light exactly over his head which shone out above the brightness of the sun, and began gradually descending towards him, until he was enveloped within it. As soon as the light appeared, the youth found himself freed from the power of the enemy that had held him bound. As the light rested upon him, he beheld within it two personages, exactly resembling each other in form and features, standing above him in the air. One of these, calling Joseph by name, and pointing to the other, said: "This is My Beloved Son, hear Him."

It gives evidence of the intellectual tenacity of Joseph Smith that in the midst of all these bewildering occurrences he held clearly in his mind the purpose for which he had come to this secluded spot, the object he had in view in seeking the Lord. As soon, therefore, as he could get sufficient self-possession to speak, he asked the Personages in whose resplendent presence he stood, which of the sects was right, and which he should join. He was answered that he must join none of them; for they were all wrong. . . .

Joseph Smith soon found that by telling the story he had excited a great deal of prejudice against himself among many professors of religion. His experience indicated how far removed men were from a sincere belief in those scriptures so frequently found upon their lips. . . .

But come what might now, his mind was satisfied as to the sectarian world. He knew they were wrong; that he was to join none of them. He had proved the testimony of James to be true. One who lacked wisdom could ask it of God, receive it, and not be upbraided. He knew now that God lived, and that man could hold visible and personal communion with Him. . . .

What a change had come to this youth in one brief hour!

How little that fair-haired boy, standing there in the unpruned forest, with the sunlight stealing through the trees about him, realized the burden placed upon his shoulders that early spring morning, by reason of the visitation he received in answer to prayer!

He has found the source of spiritual knowledge, and his life and his life's work has been broadened; but his knowledge will not bring him peace in this world,—except that peace of the soul that rejoices even in the midst of conflict—the peace "that passeth understanding": but outwardly his knowledge spells strife for him—conflict with a world. His testimony will arouse the wrath of men, and with unrelenting fury they will pursue him. Slander, outright falsehood and misrepresentation will play havoc with his reputation. Everywhere his name will be held up as evil. Derision will laugh at his message to the world. Ridicule will mock it. On every hand he will be met with the cry of "False prophet! false prophet!" Chains and the dungeon's gloom await him; mobs with murderous hate will assail him again and again; and at the last, while under the protection of the law, and the honor of a great commonwealth pledged for his safety, he will meet martyrdom in the shadow of prison walls! (*Americana*, Sept. 1909, 610–619.)

Levi Edgar Young

Levi Edgar Young (1874–1963) served in the First Council of the Seventy from 1909 until his death. His father, Seymour B. Young, served in the same council, overlapping with Levi for thirteen years. Levi's uncle was Brigham Young, president of the Church.

The vision of God the Father and the Son Jesus Christ to the boy Joseph Smith in the spring of 1820 is the one event that has ushered in a new period of the world's history. Ancient days were then left behind, and modern days began. It was the most natural thing in the world for God to reveal himself to a child whose mind was pure and who had not learned the theories of philosophy of that day. I look upon Joseph Smith as the greatest prophet of all history, for his was the work of the greatest age of man's development since the fall of Adam. (Conference Report, Apr. 1920, 160.)

Janne M. Sjodahl

Janne M. Sjodahl (1853–1939) was an editor and prolific writer for newspapers and for the Church's official magazine, the Improvement Era. *He translated three of the Church's standard works into Swedish: the Book of Mormon, the Doctrine and Covenants, and the Pearl of Great Price.*

To a thoughtful reader of the historical account of the first vision of the Prophet Joseph, his extreme youth at the time he received that glorious manifestation suggests some such questions: Is it credible that God would choose a mere boy as his messenger? Does the Almighty ignore men who have laboriously accumulated the theological and philosophical wealth of the schools—men matured in thought and well moulded by experience—when he needs a special messenger? Would he send a child in preference to a Luther, a Knox, a Wesley, a Zinzendorff, a Jonathan Edwards, a Spurgeon?

If we scan the pages of sacred history for the answer to those important queries, we find that he does. We learn that at the most important epochs in human history, God has almost invariably selected young boys for his special messengers. [Here the author gives the examples of Samuel, Jeremiah, Daniel, and John the Baptist.] . . .

We might add to these illustrations of God's choice of special representatives, the accounts of Joseph in Egypt, of David, the shepherd boy, of Timothy, the beloved companion of Paul, and of our Lord himself who, at the age of twelve years, in the Temple halls, astonished the rabbis and doctors of law with his questions and answers. They all teach the same great truth—a truth which the boys especially should endeavor to have engraved upon their hearts. They show us that when great changes in the regular course of events of human history are about to take place; when the heavens are about to be shaken and the earth to tremble, and when the waves of the sea are to heave beyond their bounds; when the Lord needs a special messenger to warn men of what is coming, he invariably selects a young boy, a child, one who is pure and uncontaminated, free from prejudices, and of sterling character and virtues. Such a boy was Joseph Smith, who was called to the prophetic office on the eve of an old dispensation and the dawn of a new, as were Samuel, Jeremiah, and John the Baptist. The Prophet Joseph is in the same class as these. And thus his very youth is strong presumptive evidence of the divine origin and authenticity of the vision.

Further impregnable evidence appears when we compare the account of this vision with the records of some of the manifestations granted to other great prophets.

Isaiah saw the Lord enthroned in glory, but it is evident that the vision was accompanied by some effort of the powers of darkness to frustrate God's plans, for the prophet exclaimed: "Woe is me! for I am undone; because I am a man of unclean lips." (Is. 6:5.) He was rescued from this influence by a divine messenger.

Daniel's experience by the river Hiddekel was similar. When he stood in the presence of a being from the other side, he fell to the ground (Dan. 10:1–18), and there was no strength in him until he had been freed from the evil power. Even his companions were seized with fear, and fled.

Saul, on the road to Damascus, in the presence of the divine light that appeared to him, fell to the ground, trembling and blinded.

John, the Revelator, fell down as dead, when he saw his glorified Master on the Isle of Patmos. (Rev. 1:17.)

Such was the experience the Prophet Joseph had on that ever memorable day of his first vision. He felt himself in the grasp of some evil power, thick darkness fell upon him, and he feared that his last hour had come. It was then that he was saved by the appearance of the divine Personages in the heavenly light. And thus, the marvelous story of the Prophet Joseph's first vision, when compared with Scripture records, bears the imprint of truth on every line.

If a modern writer of fiction had composed a story of a heavenly vision, he would, in all probability, have embellished his paragraphs with details of the features of the "angels;" with descriptions of their robes, golden crowns, harps, and especially their wings, for these things went to make up popular notions a century ago, much of it having been borrowed from Dante's and Milton's poems.

But the Prophet Joseph's narrative is not burdened with any such concepts. Rather, it is contrary to what a writer of popular fiction would have presented. It reads like a chapter of the Word of God, and it, therefore, comes to us with the irresistible force of truth. (*Improvement Era*, Apr. 1920, 488–490.)

Charles H. Hart

Charles H. Hart (1866–1934) was an attorney and judge who was called to serve in the First Council of the Seventy in 1909.

One hundred years have passed since the boy Joseph Smith declared he had been visited by two heavenly beings. The first vision was followed by many other spiritual manifestations reported by him, all of which have resulted in the birth and growth of a young, virile, vigorous Church of world-wide influence and aspirations. The Church thus launched has had a unique and striking history and has become "a marvelous work and a wonder."

After a century's test and scrutiny by a critical world, is the Church thus established still required to bear the burden of proof that Joseph Smith was a prophet, or may not unbelief be called upon to give some plausible explanation of the Prophet and his work? How is Joseph and the work inaugurated by him to be explained with inspiration or divine guidance left out of the account? Did he fabricate the religious experiences and visions reported by him? Was he a designing impostor? Was he sincere but misled by delusions or hallucinations? Or was he divinely inspired, a Prophet? Let each word and act of his come under the search light of truth and be put to the acid test. The entire record bears no evidence of insincerity. While, to begin with, many have sought to dispose of him and the work for which he stood by considering him as a willful impostor, thoughtful and well informed people concede his sincerity but seek to account for him and what he did by supposing him innocently misled. . . .

It is not to be wondered at that the best modern thought should concede Joseph's honesty. His words and acts attest fidelity. How is it that a court, or jury, is impressed with the truthfulness of the testimony of the witness and may believe him against the statement of many others? The very manner of telling the story and demeanor of the witness carry conviction. So with Joseph's story of his visions. What unprejudiced person can read his simple, candid narrative without believing him honest? It has all the evidence of an actual experience. . . .

It should be noted that the answer Joseph got was not the answer he was looking for. He asked which of all religions was right. He assumed that some one or other must be. No preconceived whim or desire on his part could account for the answer he received. If an impostor, desirous of establishing a new church, he would not have antagonized all other churches by declaiming them all wrong. The very reply received by him indicates that it was not of human origin. . . .

If the boy had not seen the vision and heard voices, why would he say to his mother, who was a Presbyterian, "I have learned for myself that Presbyterianism is not true"? Why would he lay the axe at the root of religious error unless he had been instructed as he claimed? In the same narrative he frankly confessed having fallen into errors, "and displayed the weakness of youth and the foibles of human nature." Had he been a pretender, would he have confessed having been led into temptation? Would he not have sought prestige by assuming or pretending a perfection he had not attained? . . .

The First Vision is a fitting prelude to the entire drama of the unfolding of so-called "Mormonism." It is the key to the arch of the restored Church.

It requires less credulity to believe that Joseph was inspired than to think that a boy of his age and experience could forge, so to speak, the whole stupendous structure and teachings of "Mormonism." . . .

If one considers the research required by man's learning to produce the three volumes of scripture which came through Joseph, he will realize that no boy, with Joseph's limited opportunities, could possibly have done the work without divine assistance. There are some matters that are not susceptible of successful fabrication. One is a volume of scripture. More difficult still, and less likely of attempt, would be the offer of a willful deceiver to have his work of deception affirmatively attested by the Holy Trinity in the manner requested by the Book of Mormon, to "ask God, the eternal Father, in the name of Christ, if these things are not true; and if ye shall ask with a sincere heart, with real intent, having faith in Christ, he will manifest the truth of it unto you, by the power of the Holy Ghost; and by the power of the Holy Ghost ye may know the truth of all things." (*Improvement Era*, Apr. 1920, 491–495.)

Nephi Jensen

Nephi Jensen (1876–1955) was an attorney and judge in the Salt Lake City area who wrote many missionary tracts and manuals for priesthood study. As a baby born in 1876, one hundred years after the Declaration of Independence, he was given an unusual name: Nephi United States Centennial Jensen.

[Joseph Smith's] career commenced in 1820, when he was given a vision of the Father and the Son. . . . Joseph Smith went by prayer right into the presence of God. . . . Joseph Smith, when only a boy of fourteen, saw the Maker of all, and heard the Voice that had stilled the storm and stayed the wave. . . .

Joseph Smith rediscovered the true and the living God. . . .

His first vocal prayer . . . marked the beginning of an epoch. It was the beginning of the real modern spiritual renaissance. . . .

The boy who prayed that day in the silent woodland had a heart as deep as truth, and lifted high as heaven. He had the faith that defies fate. . . . The living faith of this boy pierced the blue dome . . . and called to the earth the Majesty of heaven. . . .

Before Joseph Smith saw that vision, in answer to a prayer inspired by a specific Bible promise, the Bible had for centuries been a mere fetish. It had been a dead letter, containing the decrees and promises of God to another age. He put spirit and life into the dead letter by demonstrating that God would do today the very things he promises in his book. By the magic touch of this prophet's faith, the Bible became in fact and truth the Book of God, a compendium of his veritable promises to all men of all ages and all climes. . . .

While the divines were still graphically describing the great things God had done for his people of old, Joseph Smith fervently testified of the great things God is now doing for his people of today. He re-affirmed the promises of old and demonstrated their validity. . . .

His niche in the ages is secure. . . . The story of his triumphant faith is the most thrilling incident in modern annals. It gives hope, light, and life. It is the beacon that lights the way across the dark chasm which ages of ignorance and superstition have placed between man and God. (*Improvement Era*, Apr. 1920, 554–559.)

Susa Young Gates

Susa Young Gates (1856–1933) was a daughter of Brigham Young and Lucy Bigelow. One of her daughters married apostle John A. Widtsoe. Sister Gates was an influential editor and writer who eventually founded both the Young Woman's Journal *and the* Relief Society Magazine. *The following was written as an unsigned editorial; since Susa Young Gates was the editor of the magazine at the time, she is the presumed author.*

Which of all the sects are right? Which of all the paths, trodden by the feet of men, lead to eternal glory? These are the eternal questions asked, as some period of life, by every soul. When the youthful prophet went into the grove, on that lovely spring day of 1820, his mind was fixed only upon learning which was right of all the paths trodden along the heights to heaven. . . .

Not all may receive such as manifestation as was given to the Prophet Joseph Smith, for his question was the question of the whole race, and his answer was the answer to the whole earth. . . .

"A tree is known by its fruit," so says the Master, and the fruits of the answer which was given to the Prophet Joseph Smith are glorious beyond description. . . .

Spirit answers spirit. . . If you ask of God "Who giveth liberally and upbraideth not" you will get the answer which the Prophet

Joseph received, and you will know as I know, that God lives, that Jesus is the Christ, and that Joseph Smith had that marvelous Vision in the grove, wherein he saw with quickened eyes the   Father, who pointed to his Son and said, "This is my beloved Son, hear him." (*Relief Society Magazine,* Apr. 1920, 232–233.)

Robert L. Simpson

Robert L. Simpson (1915–2003) served as a General Authority from 1961 until his death. He also served as a mission president, temple president, and general president of the Sunday School.

[The First Vision is] the most significant singular event in the world since the resurrection of the Lord and Savior Jesus Christ. The First Vision is the very foundation of this Church, and it is my conviction that each member of this Church performs his duty in direct ratio to his personal testimony and faith in the First Vision. (*Ensign,* Jan. 1974, 87.)

Truman G. Madsen

Truman G. Madsen (1926–2009) was a professor of religion and philosophy at Brigham Young University. He was a prolific author and highly popular speaker. He was known as one of the foremost advocates of his generation of the Prophet Joseph Smith.

[In an] account of the First Vision, . . . Joseph described the descending light. In dictating the account, he . . . first used the word *fire.* That is crossed out in favor of *spirit* or *light.* The word he finally settled on and used most often was *glory.* It refers to the emanating and radiating spirit and power of God. But the word *fire* is important to notice. Orson Pratt . . . says that the young prophet expected to see "the leaves and boughs of the trees consumed." . . .

The Prophet indicates in the 1835 account that he was filled with that light, but also surrounded by it, that it filled the Grove. Then he adds, "Yet nothing consumed," perhaps indicating that he expected it to be.

The Prophet was not harmed by the experience; he was hallowed by it. Having seen the light, he now saw in it two personages, one of whom said to him, indicating the other, "This is my Beloved Son." . . .

The Prophet later taught . . . "It is the first principle of the gospel to know for a certainty the character [the personality, the attributes] of God, and to know that we may converse with him as one man converses with another." That is the testimony of Joseph Smith from beginning to end. (Madsen, *Joseph Smith, the Prophet* [1989], 10–12, 14–15.)

Richard L. Anderson

Richard L. Anderson (1926–2018) was an attorney who became a professor of Church history and doctrine at Brigham Young University. As a missionary, he authored the "Anderson Plan," an approach to teaching the gospel in set discussions that later was adapted for use by missionaries throughout the Church. He was widely recognized as a careful scholar of Joseph Smith and early Latter-day Saint history.

His account of that sacred experience is not only *his* best-documented vision of Deity, but there are few spiritual experiences in world history that rival the First Vision in rich detail and full reporting.

Joseph Smith's testimony of seeing the Father and Son towers like the arching trees of that sacred setting. . . .

The spread of the Prophet's testimony of that vision is impressive. Accounts were typeset at least thirteen times before the Martyrdom, several times at Joseph Smith's initiative. . . . Readership of these printed accounts of the First Vision must be measured in tens of thousands. . . .

Joseph Smith . . . taught from firsthand knowledge gained in many visions. . . . In an 1843 sermon, the Prophet [said], "Any person that has seen the heavens opened knows that there is three personages in the heavens holding the keys of power." . . .

The background that Joseph Smith gives for his religious quest fits very well into the known conditions of his family life and area. Yet, believing in his first vision requires a further personal step to be taken in faith. In appearing to Thomas, who doubted ten Apostles' testimony of the Resurrection, the Lord left this challenge to everyone who investigates divine visions and true prophets: "Blessed are they that have not seen, and yet have believed" (John 20:29). (*Ensign,* Apr. 1996, 20.)

Arthur Henry King

Arthur Henry King (1910–2000) was a highly regarded British poet and professor who taught at universities in Sweden. He was twice decorated by Queen Elizabeth II for his work on the British Council, which supervised educational and cultural pursuits overseas. He converted to the Church in 1966 and later taught English at Brigham Young University.

I am glad that the first thing they [the missionaries] did was to give me the pamphlet on Joseph Smith's vision. The style of the Joseph Smith story immediately struck me. He spoke to me, as soon as I read his testimony, as a great writer, transparently sincere and matter-of-fact. . . . When Joseph Smith describes his visions, he describes them not as a man who feels that he has to make the effort to persuade. He simply states what happened to him, and does it in a way that gives it credence. I am in this church because of the Joseph Smith story; my fundamental act of faith was to accept this as a remarkable document. (King, *The Abundance of the Heart* [1986], 25.)

When I was first brought to read Joseph Smith's story, I was deeply impressed. I wasn't inclined to be impressed. As a stylistician, I have spent my life being disinclined to be impressed. So when I read his story, I thought to myself, this is an extraordinary thing. This is an astonishingly matter-of-fact and cool account. This man is not trying to persuade me of anything. He doesn't feel the need to. He is stating what happened to him, and he is stating it, not enthusiastically, but in quite a matter-of-fact way. He is not trying to make me cry or feel ecstatic. That struck me, and that began to build my testimony, for I could see that this man was telling the truth. . . .

It isn't the prose of someone who is trying to work it out and make it nice. It is the prose of someone who is trying to tell it like it is, who is bending all his faculties to expressing the truth and not thinking about anything else— . . . not posturing, not posing, but just being himself. . . .

Now there is no passage in . . . any other kind of literature concerned with visions that I know of which is like this. . . . They don't compare with Joseph Smith. They attitudinize; they get into postures, contortions of mind, in expressing themselves. Not so Joseph Smith. . . .

Think of Joseph Smith as a man who speaks to our time from eternity. (King, *Arm the Children* [1998], 288–293.)

Richard Bushman

Richard Bushman (1931–present) is a historian who has taught at Harvard University, Columbia University, and BYU. A patriarch in the Church, he is the author of the award-winning biography Joseph Smith, Rough Stone Rolling *(2005).*

Those who lose faith in Christ because they have lost faith in Joseph Smith have things backward. Joseph's mission was to increase faith in Christ, not in himself. He thought of himself as one of the weak things of the world who came forth that faith might increase in the earth and that Christ's everlasting covenant might be established. He would want us to develop faith in his teachings, in Christ and the atonement, in prayer and adhesion to high moral standards, not in him as a man. He would want us to believe in the principles independent of the man. . . . We honor him as a prophet, to be sure, but as one who testified of the Savior. His revelations pointed beyond himself to Christ and the Father. I believe in Joseph Smith as a prophet of God. . . . But we must place our faith first in Christ, and believe in him apart from our faith in his messenger. Christ should be the anchor when we struggle and question.

We now benefit from having not just one but many accounts of the First Vision, each one offering a different perspective. The Vision is a powerful source of faith. It helps my faith to know that someone in our own era saw God. But we should keep in mind the Vision's purpose: it was to testify of the Lord. That Christ will come first in our faith, that he will be the foundation, that we will enjoy forgiveness and renewal through His atonement. (Speech, BYU–Hawaii, 15 Nov. 2016.)

Richard J. Maynes

Richard J. Maynes (1950–present) was CEO of a company focusing on factory automation when he was called as a General Authority Seventy in 1997.

I would like to share a sampling of truths we learn from Joseph Smith's First Vision. . . .

We learn that pondering the scriptures brings power and insight.

We learn that knowledge alone isn't enough; acting on what we know results in God's blessings. . . .

We learn that prayers are answered according to our unwavering faith and according to Heavenly Father's will.

We learn the reality of Satan's existence and that he has actual power to influence the physical world, including us. . . .

We learn that where there is light, darkness must depart.

We learn that God the Father and His Son, Jesus Christ, are two separate and distinct beings, resembling each other in features and likeness.

We learn that we are created in God's image. . . .

We learn that God knows us personally and is aware of our needs and concerns. He called Joseph by name.

We learn of the relationship between the Father and the Son. Jesus defers to His Father, and the Father communicates with mortals here upon the earth through His Son. . . .

We learn that the true Church of Jesus Christ as He originally organized it was not found upon the earth at the time of Joseph Smith. . . .

We learn insight into how God chooses His prophets. . . .

Joseph Smith's First Vision is the key to unlocking many truths that had been hidden for centuries. (*Ensign,* June 2017, 64–65.)

SELECTED SOURCES

AND ADDITIONAL READING

Allen, James B. "Eight Contemporary Accounts of Joseph Smith's First Vision—What Do We Learn from Them?" *Improvement Era*, Apr. 1970, 4–13.

———. "Emergence of a Fundamental: The Expanding Role of Joseph Smith's First Vision in Mormon Religious Thought." *Journal of Mormon History* 7 (1980): 43–61.

———. "The Significance of Joseph Smith's 'First Vision' in Mormon Thought." In *Exploring the First Vision*. Edited by Samuel Alonzo Dodge and Steven C. Harper. Provo, UT: Religious Studies Center, Brigham Young University, 2012, 283–306.

———, and John W. Welch. "The Appearance of the Father and the Son to Joseph Smith in 1820." In *Opening the Heavens: Accounts of Divine Manifestations, 1820–1844*, 35–75. Edited by John W. Welch. Deseret Book and Brigham Young University, 2005.

Anderson, Richard L. "Circumstantial Confirmation of the First Vision Through Reminiscences." *BYU Studies* 9, no. 3 (Spring 1969): 1–27.

———. "Joseph Smith's Testimony of the First Vision." *Ensign*, Apr. 1996, 10–21.

Asay, Carlos E. "'Oh, How Lovely Was the Morning!': Joseph Smith's First Prayer and the First Vision." *Ensign*, Apr. 1995, 44–49.

Backman, Milton V., Jr. "Confirming Witnesses of the First Vision." *Ensign,* Jan. 1986, 32–37.

———. *Eyewitness Accounts of the Restoration.* Salt Lake City: Deseret Book, 1986.

———. *Joseph Smith's First Vision: Confirming Evidences and Contemporary Accounts.* 2nd ed. Salt Lake City: Bookcraft, 1980.

———. *Joseph Smith's First Vision: The First Vision in its Historical Context.* 2nd ed. rev. Salt Lake City: Bookcraft, 1980.

———. "Joseph Smith's Recitals of the First Vision." *Ensign,* Jan. 1985, 8–17.

———. "Verification of the 1838 Account of the First Vision." In *The Pearl of Great Price: Revelations from God,* 197–212. Edited by H. Donl Peterson and Charles D. Tate Jr. Provo, UT: Religious Studies Center, Brigham Young University, 1989.

Brown, Matthew B. *A Pillar of Light: The History and Message of the First Vision.* American Fork, UT: Covenant Communications, 2009.

Cheesman, Paul R. "An Analysis of the Accounts Relating to Joseph Smith's Early Visions." M.A. thesis. Provo, UT: Brigham Young University, 1965.

Dodge, Samuel Alonzo, and Steven C. Harper. *Exploring the First Vision.* Provo, UT: Religious Studies Center, 2012.

Harper, Steven C. *First Vision: Memory and Mormon Origins.* New York: Oxford, 2019.

———. *Joseph Smith's First Vision: A Guide to the Historical Accounts.* Salt Lake City: Deseret Book, 2012.

———. "Listening to Joseph Smith's First Vision." *Meridian Magazine,* 24 Jan. 2013, https://ldsmag.com/article-1-12123/.

———. "Suspicion or Trust: Reading the Accounts of Joseph Smith's First Vision." In *No Weapon Shall Prosper: New Light on Sensitive Issues,* 63–75. Edited by Robert L. Millet. Provo, UT: Religious Studies Center, Brigham Young University; Salt Lake City: Deseret Book, 2011.

Improvement Era. Apr. 1920, 467–575.

Jessee, Dean C. "The Earliest Documented Accounts of Joseph Smith's First Vision." In *Opening the Heavens: Accounts of Divine Manifestations, 1820–1844,* 1–33. Edited by John W. Welch.

Deseret Book and Brigham Young University, 2005.

———. "The Early Accounts of Joseph Smith's First Vision." *BYU Studies* 9, no. 3 (Spring 1969): 275–294.

———. "Joseph Smith Jr.—in His Own Words, Part 1." *Ensign,* Dec. 1984, 22–31.

"Joseph Smith's Accounts of the First Vision," josephsmith-papers.org/articles/primary-accounts-of-first-vision.

Maynes, Richard J. "The First Vision: Key to Truth." *Ensign,* June 2017, 60–65.

"Primary Accounts of Joseph Smith's First Vision of Deity," josephsmithpapers.org/site/accounts-of-the-first-vision.

Widtsoe, John A. "The Challenge of the First Vision." In *Joseph Smith: Seeker After Truth, Prophet of God,* 5–9. Salt Lake City: Book-craft, 1951.